Save and grow

A policymaker's guide to the sustainable intensification of smallholder crop production

Published by Arrangement with the
FOOD AND AGRICULTURE ORGANIZATION OF THE UNITED NATIONS
by
SYNERGY
Synergy Books India
(A Unit of M/s Bookwell Publications)
New Delhi (India)

First Indian Reprint Edition 2013 by

SYNERGY BOOKS INDIA
(A Unit of M/s Bookwell Publications)
24/4800 Ansari Road, Daryaganj,
New Delhi-110002
Phone: 23268786, 23257264
Fax: 23281315
Email: synergybooksindia@gmail.com/bookwell@vsnl.net
Website: www.synergybooksindia.com

Printed at Mudrak, 30 A Patparganj, Delhi-110091

ISBN : 978-93-82059-04-2

a) "This book was originally published in (year) by the Food and Agriculture Organization of the United Nations (FAO) as (title)".

b) "The designations employed and the presentation material in this information product do not imply the expression of any opinion whatsoever on the part of the Food and Agriculture Organization of the United Nations concerning the legal or development status of any country, territory, city or area of its authorities, or concerning the delimitation of its frontiers or boundaries. The mention of specific companies or products of manufacturers, whether or not these have been patented, does not imply that these have been endorsed or recommended by the Food and Agriculture Organization of the United Nations in preference to others of a similar nature that are not mentioned.

The views expressed in this publication are those of the author(s) and do not necessarily reflect the views of the Food and Agriculture Organization of the United Nations.

Foreword

The Green Revolution in agriculture, which swept much of the developing world during the 1960s, saved an estimated one billion people from famine. Thanks to high-yielding crop varieties, irrigation, agrochemicals and modern management techniques, farmers in developing countries increased food production from 800 million tonnes to more than 2.2 billion tonnes between 1961 and 2000. Intensive crop production helped to reduce the number of undernourished, drive rural development and prevent the destruction of natural ecosystems to make way for extensive farming. Those achievements came at a cost. In many countries, decades of intensive cropping have degraded fertile land and depleted groundwater, provoked pest upsurges, eroded biodiversity, and polluted air, soil and water. As the world population rises to a projected 9.2 billion in 2050, we have no option but to further intensify crop production. But the yield growth rate of major cereals is declining, and farmers face a series of unprecedented, intersecting challenges: increasing competition for land and water, rising fuel and fertilizer prices, and the impact of climate change.

The present paradigm of intensive crop production cannot meet the challenges of the new millennium. In order to grow, agriculture must learn to *save*. Consider, for example, the hidden cost of repeated ploughing. By disrupting soil structure, intensive tillage leads to loss of nutrients, moisture and productivity. More farmers could save natural resources, time and money if they adopted conservation agriculture (CA), which minimizes tillage, protects the soil surface, and alternates cereals with soil-enriching legumes. Those simple practices help to reduce crops' water needs by 30 percent and the energy costs of production by up to 60 percent. In trials in southern Africa, they increased maize yields six-fold. Combining CA with precision irrigation produces more crops from fewer drops. Farmers can reduce the need for fertilizers by adopting "precision placement", which doubles the amount of nutrients absorbed by plants. By using insecticides wisely, they can save pest predators and disrupt the cycle of pest resistance. Economizing on agrochemicals and building healthy agro-ecosystems would enable low-income farm families in developing countries – some 2.5 billion people – to maximize yields and invest the savings in their health and education.

This new paradigm of agriculture is sustainable crop production intensification (SCPI), which can be summed up in the words "save and grow". Sustainable intensification means a productive agriculture that conserves and enhances natural resources. It uses an ecosystem approach that draws on nature's contribution to crop growth – soil organic matter, water flow regulation, pollination and natural predation of pests – and applies appropriate external inputs at the right time, in the right amount. "Save and grow" farming systems offer proven productivity, economic and environmental benefits. A review of agricultural development in 57 low-income countries found that ecosystem farming led to average yield increases of almost 80 percent. Conservation agriculture, which is practised on more than 100 million hectares worldwide, contributes to climate change mitigation by sequestering in soil millions of tonnes of carbon a year.

SCPI represents a major shift from the homogeneous model of crop production to knowledge-intensive, often location-specific, farming systems. Its application will require significant support to farmers in testing new practices and adapting technologies. Governments will need to strengthen national programmes for plant genetic resources conservation, plant breeding and seed distribution in order to deploy improved crop varieties that are resilient to climate change and use nutrients, water and external inputs more efficiently. Fundamental changes are also required in agricultural development strategies. Policymakers must provide incentives for adoption of SCPI, such as rewarding good management of agro-ecosystems. Developed countries should support sustainable intensification by increasing considerably the flow of external assistance to, and investment in, agriculture in the developing world.

Sustainable intensification of smallholder crop production is one of FAO's strategic objectives. Our aim over the next 15 years is to assist developing countries in adopting "save and grow" policies and approaches. This book provides a toolkit of adaptable farming systems, technologies and practices, and explores the policies and the institutional arrangements that will support the large-scale implementation of SCPI.

Jacques Diouf
Director-General
Food and Agriculture Organization
of the United Nations

Contents

Foreword **iii**
Acknowledgements **vi**
Overview **vii**

Chapter 1: The challenge **1**
Chapter 2: Farming systems **15**
Chapter 3: Soil health **27**
Chapter 4: Crops and varieties **39**
Chapter 5: Water management **51**
Chapter 6: Plant protection **65**
Chapter 7: Policies and institutions **77**

Sources **95**
Abbreviations **102**

Acknowledgements

This book was produced under the direction of Shivaji Pandey, Director of FAO's Plant Production and Protection Division. Guidance was provided by a steering committee and a technical advisory group. Final technical editing was done by Mangala Rai (President of the National Academy of Agricultural Sciences, India), Timothy Reeves (former Director-General of the International Maize and Wheat Improvement Center), and Shivaji Pandey.

Authors

Lead authors:
Linda Collette (FAO), Toby Hodgkin (Bioversity International), Amir Kassam (University of Reading, UK), Peter Kenmore (FAO), Leslie Lipper (FAO), Christian Nolte (FAO), Kostas Stamoulis (FAO), Pasquale Steduto (FAO)
Collaborators:
Manuela Allara (FAO), Doyle Baker (FAO), Hasan Bolkan (Campbell Soup Co., USA), Jacob Burke (FAO), Romina Cavatassi (FAO), Mark L. Davis (FAO), Hartwig De Haen (University of Göttingen, Germany), João Carlos de Moraes Sá (Universidade Estadual de Ponta Grossa, Brazil), Marjon Fredrix (FAO), Theodor Friedrich (FAO), Kakoli Ghosh (FAO), Jorge Hendrichs (FAO/IAEA), Barbara Herren (FAO), Francesca Mancini (FAO), Philip Mikos (EC), Thomas Osborn (FAO), Jules Pretty (University of Essex, UK), David Radcliffe (EC), Timothy Reeves (Timothy G. Reeves and Associates P/L, Australia), Mike Robson (FAO), Amit Roy (IFDC), Francis Shaxson (Tropical Agriculture Association, UK), Hugh Turral (RPF P/L, Australia), Harry Van der Wulp (FAO)

Steering committee

Chair: Shivaji Pandey (FAO)
Rodney Cooke (IFAD), Dennis Garrity (ICRAF), Toby Hodgkin (Bioversity International), Philip Mikos (EC), Mohammad Saeid Noori Naeini (Iran), Timothy Reeves (Timothy G. Reeves and Associates P/L, Australia), Amit Roy (IFDC), M. S. Swaminathan (M. S. Swaminathan Research Foundation, India)

Technical advisory group

Hasan Bolkan (Campbell Soup Co., USA), Anne-Marie Izac (Future Harvest Alliance, France), Louise Jackson (University of California, Davis, USA), Janice Jiggins (Wageningen University and Research Centre, the Netherlands), Patrick Mulvany (Intermediate Technology Development Group, UK), Wayne Powell (Aberystwyth University, UK), Jessie Sainz Binamira (Department of Agriculture, the Philippines), Bob Watson (University of East Anglia, UK)

Overview

1. The challenge

To feed a growing world population, we have no option but to intensify crop production. But farmers face unprecedented constraints. In order to grow, agriculture must learn to save.

The Green Revolution led to a quantum leap in food production and bolstered world food security. In many countries, however, intensive crop production has depleted agriculture's natural resource base, jeopardizing future productivity. In order to meet projected demand over the next 40 years, farmers in the developing world must double food production, a challenge made even more daunting by the combined effects of climate change and growing competition for land, water and energy. This book presents a new paradigm: sustainable crop production intensification (SCPI), which produces more from the same area of land while conserving resources, reducing negative impacts on the environment and enhancing natural capital and the flow of ecosystem services.

2. Farming systems

Crop production intensification will be built on farming systems that offer a range of productivity, socio-economic and environmental benefits to producers and to society at large.

The ecosystem approach to crop production regenerates and sustains the health of farmland. Farming systems for SCPI will be based on conservation agriculture practices, the use of good seed of high-yielding adapted varieties, integrated pest management, plant nutrition based on healthy soils, efficient water management, and the integration of crops, pastures, trees and livestock. The very nature of sustainable production systems is dynamic: they should offer farmers many possible combinations of practices to choose from and adapt, according to their local production conditions and constraints. Such systems are knowledge-intensive. Policies for SCPI should build capacity through extension approaches such as farmer field schools, and facilitate local production of specialized farm tools.

3. Soil health

Agriculture must, literally, return to its roots by rediscovering the importance of healthy soil, drawing on natural sources of plant nutrition, and using mineral fertilizer wisely.

Soils rich in biota and organic matter are the foundation of increased crop productivity. The best yields are achieved when nutrients come from a mix of mineral fertilizers and natural sources, such as manure and nitrogen-fixing crops and trees. Judicious use of mineral fertilizers saves money and ensures that nutrients reach the plant and do not pollute air, soil and waterways. Policies to promote soil health should encourage conservation agriculture and mixed crop-livestock and agro-forestry systems that enhance soil fertility. They should remove incentives that encourage mechanical tillage and the wasteful use of fertilizers, and transfer to farmers precision approaches such as urea deep placement and site-specific nutrient management.

4. Crops and varieties

Farmers will need a genetically diverse portfolio of improved crop varieties that are suited to a range of agro-ecosystems and farming practices, and resilient to climate change.

Genetically improved cereal varieties accounted for some 50 percent of the increase in yields over the past few decades. Plant breeders must achieve similar results in the future. However, timely delivery to farmers of high-yielding varieties requires big improvements in the system that connects plant germplasm collections, plant breeding and seed delivery. Over the past century, about 75 percent of plant genetic resources (PGR) has been lost and a third of today's diversity could disappear by 2050. Increased support to PGR collection, conservation and utilization is crucial. Funding is also needed to revitalize public plant breeding programmes. Policies should help to link formal and farmer-saved seed systems, and foster the emergence of local seed enterprises.

5. Water management

Sustainable intensification requires smarter, precision technologies for irrigation and farming practices that use ecosystem approaches to conserve water.

Cities and industries are competing intensely with agriculture for the use of water. Despite its high productivity, irrigation is under growing pressure to reduce its environmental impact, including soil salinization and nitrate contamination of aquifers. Knowledge-based precision irrigation that provides reliable and flexible water application, along with deficit irrigation and wastewater-reuse, will be a major platform for sustainable intensification. Policies will need to eliminate perverse subsidies that encourage farmers to waste water. In rainfed areas, climate change threatens millions of small farms. Increasing rainfed productivity will depend on the use of improved, drought tolerant varieties and management practices that save water.

6. Plant protection

Pesticides kill pests, but also pests' natural enemies, and their overuse can harm farmers, consumers and the environment. The first line of defence is a healthy agro-ecosystem.

In well managed farming systems, crop losses to insects can often be kept to an acceptable minimum by deploying resistant varieties, conserving predators and managing crop nutrient levels to reduce insect reproduction. Recommended measures against diseases include use of clean planting material, crop rotations to suppress pathogens, and eliminating infected host plants. Effective weed management entails timely manual weeding, minimized tillage and the use of surface residues. When necessary, lower risk synthetic pesticides should be used for targeted control, in the right quantity and at the right time. Integrated pest management can be promoted through farmer field schools, local production of biocontrol agents, strict pesticide regulations, and removal of pesticide subsidies.

7. Policies and institutions

To encourage smallholders to adopt sustainable crop production intensification, fundamental changes are needed in agricultural development policies and institutions.

First, farming needs to be profitable: smallholders must be able to afford inputs and be sure of earning a reasonable price for their crops. Some countries protect income by fixing minimum prices for commodities; others are exploring "smart subsidies" on inputs, targeted to low-income producers. Policymakers also need to devise incentives for small-scale farmers to use natural resources wisely – for example, through payments for environmental services and land tenure that entitles them to benefit from increases in the value of natural capital – and reduce the transaction costs of access to credit, which is urgently needed for investment. In many countries, regulations are needed to protect farmers from unscrupulous dealers selling bogus seed and other inputs. Major investment will be needed to rebuild research and technology transfer capacity in developing countries in order to provide farmers with appropriate technologies and to enhance their skills through farmer field schools.

Chapter 1

The challenge

To feed a growing world population, we have no option but to intensify crop production. But farmers face unprecedented constraints. In order to grow, agriculture must learn to save

The history of agriculture can be seen as a long process of intensification[1], as society sought to meet its ever growing needs for food, feed and fibre by raising crop productivity. Over millennia, farmers selected for cultivation plants that were higher yielding and more resistant to drought and disease, built terraces to conserve soil and canals to distribute water to their fields, replaced simple hoes with oxen-drawn ploughs, and used animal manure as fertilizer and sulphur against pests.

Agricultural intensification in the twentieth century represented a paradigm shift from traditional farming systems, based largely on the management of natural resources and ecosystem services, to the application of biochemistry and engineering to crop production. Following the same model that had revolutionized manufacturing, agriculture in the industrialized world adopted mechanization, standardization, labour-saving technologies and the use of chemicals to feed and protect crops. Great increases in productivity have been achieved through the use of heavy farm equipment and machinery powered by fossil fuel, intensive tillage, high-yielding crop varieties, irrigation, manufactured inputs, and ever increasing capital intensity[2].

The intensification of crop production in the developing world began in earnest with the Green Revolution. Beginning in the 1950s and expanding through the 1960s, changes were seen in crop varieties and agricultural practices worldwide[3]. The production model, which focused initially on the introduction of improved, higher-yielding varieties of wheat, rice and maize in high potential areas[4, 5] relied upon and promoted homogeneity: genetically uniform varieties grown with high levels of complementary inputs, such as irrigation, fertilizers and pesticides, which often replaced natural capital. Fertilizers replaced soil quality management, while herbicides provided an alternative to crop rotations as a means of controlling weeds[6].

The Green Revolution is credited, especially in Asia, with having jump-started economies, alleviated rural poverty, saved large areas of fragile land from conversion to extensive farming, and helped to avoid a Malthusian outcome to growth in world population. Between 1975 and 2000, cereal yields in South Asia increased by more than 50 percent, while poverty declined by 30 percent[7]. Over the past half-century, since the advent of the Green Revolution, world annual production of cereals, coarse grains, roots and tubers, pulses and oil crops has grown from 1.8 billion tonnes to 4.6 billion tonnes[8]. Growth

Indicators of global crop production intensification, 1961-2007
Index (1961=100)

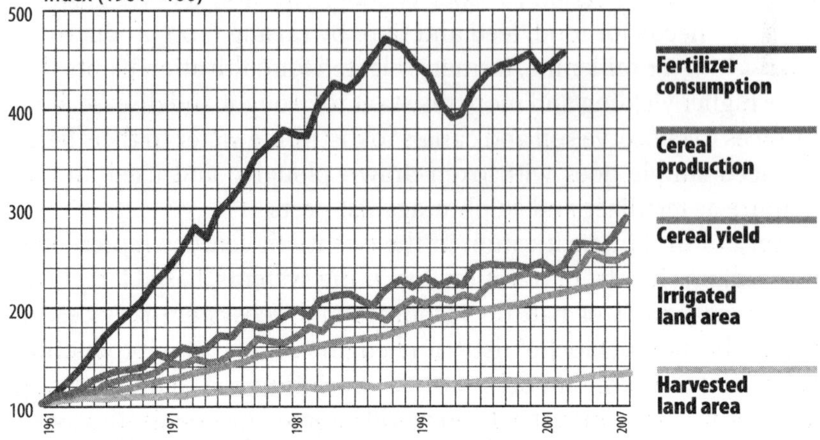

FAO. 2011.
FAOSTAT statistical database
(http://faostat.fao.org/).

World production of major crops*, 1961-2009 (billion tonnes)

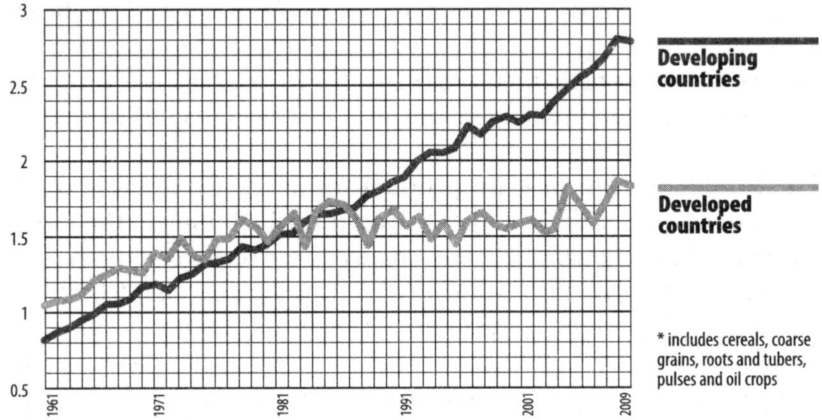

FAO. 2011.
FAOSTAT statistical database
(http://faostat.fao.org/).

Undernourished in developing world population, 1969-71 to 2010
(percent)

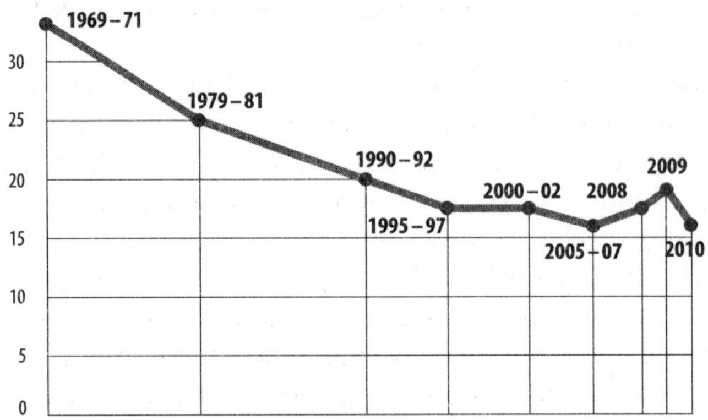

FAO. 2010. *The State of Food Insecurity in the World: Addressing food insecurity in protracted crises.* Rome.

in cereal yields and lower cereal prices significantly reduced food insecurity in the 1970s and 1980s, when the number of undernourished actually fell, despite relatively rapid population growth. Overall, the proportion of undernourished in the world population declined from 26 percent to 14 percent between 1969-1971 and 2000-2002[9].

A gathering storm

It is now recognized that those enormous gains in agricultural production and productivity were often accompanied by negative effects on agriculture's natural resource base, so serious that they jeopardize its productive potential in the future. "Negative externalities" of intensification include land degradation, salinization of irrigated areas, over-extraction of groundwater, the buildup of pest resistance and the erosion of biodiversity. Agriculture has also damaged the wider environment through, for example, deforestation, the emission of greenhouse gases and nitrate pollution of water bodies[10, 11].

It is also clear that current food production and distribution systems are failing to feed the world. The total number of undernourished people in 2010 was estimated at 925 million, higher than it was 40 years ago, and in the developing world the prevalence of undernourishment stands at 16 percent[12]. About 75 percent of those worst affected live in rural areas of developing countries, with livelihoods that depend directly or indirectly on agriculture[13]. They include many of the world's half a billion low-income smallholder farmers and their families who produce 80 percent of the food supply in developing countries. Together, smallholders use and manage more than 80 percent of farmland – and similar proportions of other natural resources – in Asia and Africa[14].

Over the next 40 years, world food security will be threatened by a number of developments. The Earth's population is projected to increase from an estimated 6.9 billion in 2010 to around 9.2 billion in 2050, with growth almost entirely in less developed regions; the highest growth rates are foreseen in the least developed countries[15]. By then, about 70 percent of the global population will be urban, compared to 50 percent today. If trends continue, urbanization and income growth in developing countries will lead to higher meat

United Nations.
World urbanization prospects, the 2009 revision population database (http://esa.un.org/wup2009/unup/).

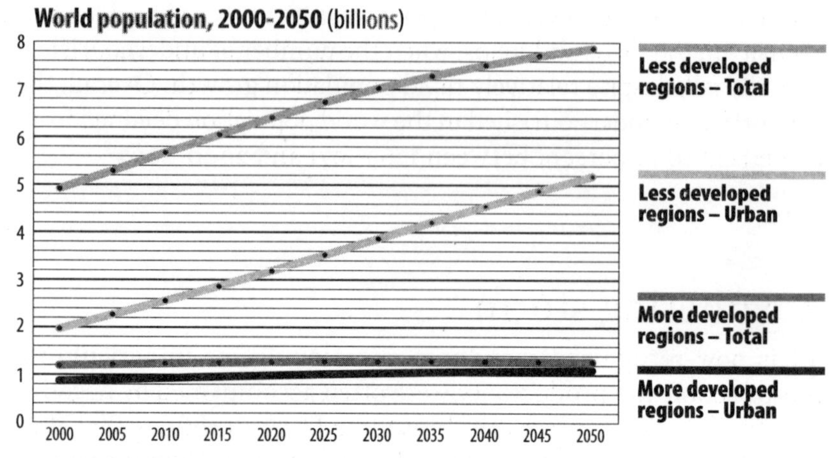

FAO. 2011.
FAOSTAT statistical database (http://faostat.fao.org/).

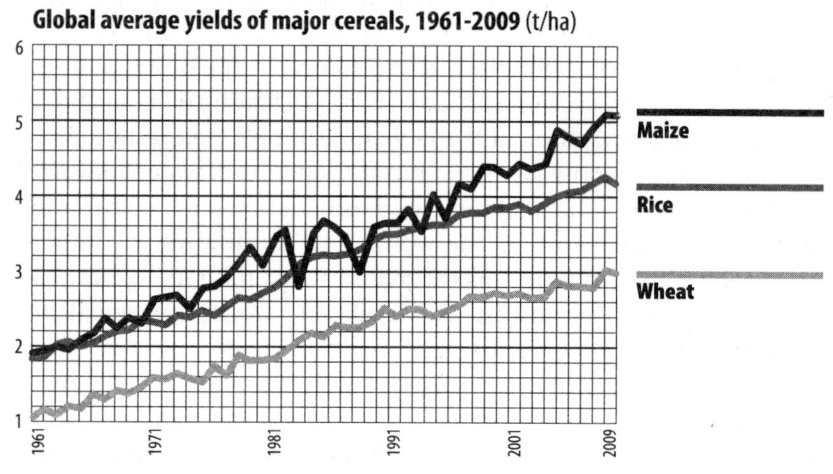

IFDC,
derived from FAOSTAT statistical database (http://faostat.fao.org/).

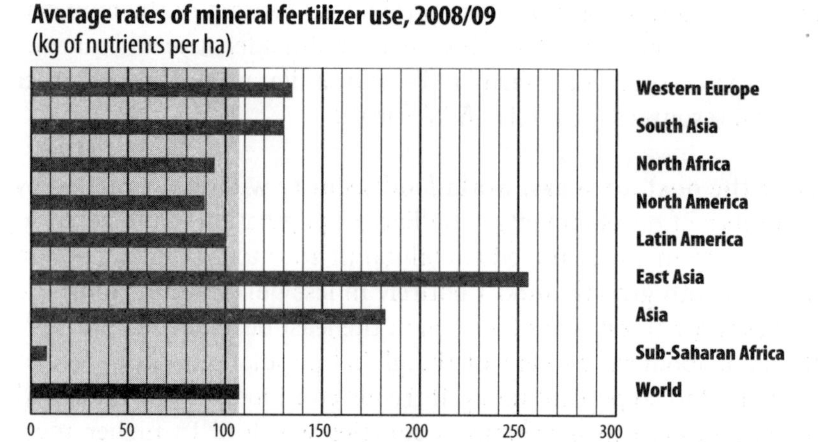

consumption, which will drive increased demand for cereals to feed livestock. The use of agricultural commodities in the production of biofuels will also continue to grow. By 2020, industrialized countries may be consuming 150 kg of maize per head per year in the form of ethanol – similar to rates of cereal food consumption in developing countries[16].

Those changes in demand will drive the need for significant increases in production of all major food and feed crops. FAO projections suggest that by 2050 agricultural production must increase by 70 percent globally – and by almost 100 percent in developing countries – in order to meet food demand alone, excluding additional demand for agricultural products used as feedstock in biofuel production. That is equivalent to an extra billion tonnes of cereals and 200 million tonnes of meat to be produced annually by 2050, compared with production between 2005 and 2007[10].

In most developing countries, there is little room for expansion of arable land. Virtually no spare land is available in South Asia and the Near East/North Africa. Where land is available, in sub-Saharan Africa and Latin America, more than 70 percent suffers from soil and terrain constraints. Between 2015 and 2030, therefore, an estimated 80 percent of the required food production increases will have to come from intensification in the form of yield increases and higher cropping intensities[17]. However, the rates of growth in yield of the major food crops – rice, wheat and maize – are all declining. Annual growth in wheat yields slipped from about 5 percent a year in 1980 to 2 percent in 2005; yield growth in rice and maize fell from more than 3 percent to around 1 percent in the same period[18]. In Asia, the degradation of soils and the buildup of toxins in intensive paddy systems have raised concerns that the slowdown in yield growth reflects a deteriorating crop-growing environment[4].

The declining quality of the land and water resources available for crop production has major implications for the future. The United Nations Environment Programme (UNEP) has estimated that unsustainable land use practices result in global net losses of cropland productivity averaging 0.2 percent a year[19]. Resource degradation reduces the productivity of inputs, such as fertilizer and irrigation. In the coming years, intensification of crop production will be required increasingly in more marginal production areas with less reliable production conditions, including lower soil quality, more limited access to water, and less favourable climates.

Efforts to increase crop production will take place under rapidly changing, often unpredictable, environmental and socio-economic conditions. One of the most crucial challenges is the need to adapt to climate change, which – through alterations in temperature, precipitation and pest incidence – will affect which crops can be grown and when, as well as their potential yields[13]. In the near term, climate variability and extreme weather shocks are projected to increase, affecting all regions[20-23], with negative impacts on yield growth and food security particularly in sub-Saharan Africa and South Asia in the period up to 2030[24]. Agriculture (including deforestation) accounts for about one third of greenhouse gas emissions; for this reason it must contribute significantly to climate change mitigation[21]. While crops can be adapted to changing environments, the need to reduce emissions will increasingly challenge conventional, resource-intensive agricultural systems[3].

Another significant source of future uncertainty is the price and availability of energy, needed to power farm operations and for the production of key inputs, principally fertilizer. As the supply of fossil fuels declines, their prices rise, driving up input prices, and consequently agricultural production costs. Fossil fuels can no longer be the sole source of energy for increasing productivity. Energy sources will have to be considerably diversified to reduce the cost of fuel for further agricultural intensification.

The challenge of meeting future demand for food in a sustainable manner is made even more daunting, therefore, by the combined effects of climate change, energy scarcity and resource degradation. The food price spike of 2008 and the surge in food prices to record levels early in 2011 portend rising and more frequent threats to world food security[25]. After examining a wide range of plausible futures – economic, demographic and climate – the International Food Policy Research Institute (IFPRI) estimated that the period 2010 to 2050 could see real price increases of 59 percent for wheat, 78 percent for rice and 106 percent for maize. The study concluded that rising prices reflect the "relentless underlying pressures on the world food system", driven by population and income growth and by reduced productivity[26].

The risk of persistent, long-term food insecurity remains most acute in low-income developing countries. The rate at which pressures are mounting on resources and the broader environment from the expansion and intensification of agriculture will be concentrated increasingly in countries with low levels of food consumption, high population growth rates and often poor agricultural resource endowments[27]. There, smallholders, who are highly dependent on ecosystem goods and services to provide food, fuel and fibre for their families and the market, are inherently more vulnerable to the declining quality and quantity of natural resources and changes in climate[14]. Without action to improve the productivity of smallholder agriculture in these countries, it is unlikely that the first Millennium Development Goal – with its targets of reducing by half the proportion of people living in hunger and poverty by 2015 – can be achieved.

Another paradigm shift

Given the current and burgeoning future challenges to our food supply and to the environment, ***sustainable*** intensification of agricultural production is emerging as a major priority for policy-makers[28] and international development partners[7, 14]. Sustainable intensification has been defined as producing more from the same area of land while reducing negative environmental impacts and increasing contributions to natural capital and the flow of environmental services[29].

Sustainable crop production intensification (or SCPI) is FAO's first strategic objective. In order to achieve that objective, FAO has endorsed the "ecosystem approach" in agricultural management[30]. Essentially, the ecosystem approach uses inputs, such as land, water, seed and fertilizer, to complement the natural processes that support plant growth, including pollination, natural predation for pest control, and the action of soil biota that allows plants to access nutrients[31].

There is now widespread awareness that an ecosystem approach must underpin intensification of crop production. A major study of the future of food and farming up to 2050 has called for substantial changes throughout the world's food system, including sustainable intensification to simultaneously raise yields, increase efficiency in the use of inputs and reduce the negative environmental effects of food production[32]. The International Assessment of Agricultural Knowledge, Science and Technology for Development (IAASTD) also called for a shift from current farming practices to sustainable agriculture systems capable of providing both significant productivity increases and enhanced ecosystem services[33].

Assessments in developing countries have shown how farm practices that conserve resources improve the supply of environmental services and increase productivity. A review of agricultural development projects in 57 low-income countries found that more efficient use of water, reduced use of pesticides and improvements in soil health had led to average crop yield increases of 79 percent[34]. Another study concluded that agricultural systems that conserve ecosystem services by using practices such as conservation tillage, crop diversification, legume intensification and biological pest control, perform as well as intensive, high-input systems[35, 36].

Sustainable crop production intensification, when effectively implemented and supported, will provide the "win-win" outcomes required to meet the dual challenges of feeding the world's population and saving the planet. SCPI will allow countries to plan, develop and manage agricultural production in a manner that addresses society's needs and aspirations, without jeopardizing the right of future generations to enjoy the full range of environmental goods and services. One example of a win-win situation – that benefits farmers as well as the environment – would be a reduction in the overuse of inputs such as mineral fertilizers along with increases in productivity.

As well as bringing multiple benefits to food security and the environment, sustainable intensification has much to offer small farmers and their families – who make up more than one-third of the global population – by enhancing their productivity, reducing costs, building resilience to stress and strengthening their capacity to manage risk[14]. Reduced spending on agricultural inputs will free resources for investment in farms and farm families' food, health and education[29]. Increases to farmers' net incomes will be achieved at lower environmental cost, thus delivering both private and public benefits[31].

Key principles

Ecosystem approaches to agricultural intensification have emerged over the past two decades as farmers began to adopt sustainable practices, such as integrated pest management and conservation agriculture, often building on traditional techniques. Sustainable crop production intensification is characterized by a more systemic approach to managing natural resources, and is founded on a set of science-based environmental, institutional and social principles.

Environmental principles

The ecosystem approach needs to be applied throughout the food chain in order to increase efficiencies and strengthen the global food system. At the scale of cropping systems, management should be based on biological processes and integration of a range of plant species, as well as the judicious use of external inputs such as fertilizers and pesticides. SCPI is based on agricultural production systems and management practices that are described in the following chapters. They include:

- maintaining healthy soil to enhance crop nutrition;
- cultivating a wider range of species and varieties in associations, rotations and sequences;
- using well adapted, high-yielding varieties and good quality seeds;
- integrated management of insect pests, diseases and weeds;
- efficient water management.

For optimal impact on productivity and sustainability, SCPI will need to be applicable to a wide variety of farming systems, and adaptable to specific agro-ecological and socio-economic contexts. It is recognized that appropriate management practices are critical to realizing the benefits of ecosystem services while reducing disservices from agricultural activities[36].

Institutional principles

It is unrealistic to hope that farmers will adopt sustainable practices only because they are more environmentally friendly. Translating the environmental principles into large-scale, coordinated programmes of action will require institutional support at both national and local levels. For governments, the challenge is to improve coordination and communication across all subsectors of agriculture, from production to processing and marketing. Mechanisms must be developed to strengthen institutional linkages in order to improve the formulation of policies and strategies for SCPI, and to sustain the scaling up of pilot studies, farmers' experiences, and local and traditional knowledge.

At the local level, farmer organizations have an important role to play in facilitating access to resources – especially land, water, credit and knowledge – and ensuring that the voice of farmers is heard[37]. Smallholder farmers also need access to efficient and equitable markets, and incentives that encourage them to manage other ecosystem services besides food production. Farmer uptake of SCPI will depend on concrete benefits, such as increased income and reduced labour requirements. If the economic system reflects costs appropriately – including the high environmental cost of unsustainable practices – the equation will shift in favour of the adoption of SCPI.

Social principles

Sustainable intensification has been described as a process of "social learning", since the knowledge required is generally greater than that used in most conventional farming approaches[14]. SCPI will require, therefore, significant strengthening of extension services, from both traditional and non-traditional sources, to support its adoption by farmers. One of the most successful approaches for training farmers to incorporate sustainable natural resource management practices into their farming systems is the extension methodology known as farmer field schools[38] (FFS)*.

Mobilizing social capital for SCPI will require people's participation in local decision-making, ensuring decent and fair working conditions in agriculture, and – above all – the recognition of the critical role of women in agriculture. Studies in sub-Saharan Africa overwhelmingly support the conclusion that differences in farm yields between men and women are caused primarily by differences in access to resources and extension services. Closing the gender gap in agriculture can improve productivity, with important additional benefits, such as raising the incomes of female farmers and increasing the availability of food[39].

* Pioneered in Southeast Asia in the late 1980s as part of an FAO regional programme on integrated pest management for rice, the FFS approach has been adopted in more than 75 countries and now covers a wide and growing range of crops and crop production issues.

The way forward

With policy support and adequate funding, sustainable crop production intensification could be implemented over large production areas, in a relatively short period of time. The challenge facing policymakers is to find effective ways of scaling up sustainable intensification so that eventually hundreds of millions of people can benefit[32]. In practical terms, the key implementation stages include:

- Assessing potential negative impacts on the agro-ecosystem of current agricultural practices. This might involve quantitative assessment for specific indicators, and reviewing plans with stakeholders at the district or provincial levels.
- Deciding at national level which production systems are potentially unsustainable and therefore require priority attention, and which areas of ecosystem sustainability (e.g. soil health, water quality, conservation of biodiversity) are priorities for intervention.
- Working with farmers to validate and adapt technologies that address those priorities in an integrated way, and use the experience to prepare plans for investment and to develop appropriate institutions and policies.
- Rolling out programmes (with technical assistance and enabling policies) based on the approaches and technologies described in this book.
- Monitoring, evaluating and reviewing progress, and making on-course adjustments where required.

This process can be iterative, and in any case relies on managing the interplay between national policy and institutions, on the one hand, and the local experience of farmers and consumers on the other. Monitoring of key ecosystem variables can help adjust and fine-tune SCPI initiatives.

In preparing programmes, policymakers may need to consider issues that affect both SCPI and the development of the agricultural sector as a whole. There is a risk, for example, that policies that seek to achieve economies of scale through value chain development and consolidation of land holdings may exclude smallholders from the process, or reduce their access to productive resources. Improving transport infrastructure will facilitate farmers' access to supplies of fertilizer and seed, both critical for SCPI, and to markets. Given the high rate of losses in the food chain – an estimated 30 to 40 percent of food is lost to waste and spoilage worldwide – investment in processing, storage and cold chain facilities will enable farmers to capture more value from their production. Policymakers can also promote small farmers' participation in SCPI by improving their access to production and market information through modern information and communication technology.

International instruments, conventions, and treaties relevant to SCPI may need to be harmonized, improved and implemented more effectively. That will require collaboration between international organizations concerned with rural development and natural resources* as well as governments, civil society organizations and farmer associations. Capacity is urgently needed to implement, at regional, national and local levels, internationally agreed governance arrangements**.

In addition, a number of non-legally binding international instruments embody cooperation for the enhancement and sustainable use of natural resources. They include guidelines and codes – such as the International Code of Conduct on the Distribution and Use of Pesticides – which aim at improving management of transboundary threats to production, the environment and human health. Finally, the United Nations Special Rapporteur on the Right to Food has produced guiding principles on land leasing and speculation in food commodity markets, and called for the scaling-up of ecological approaches in agriculture.

* Such as: FAO, the International Fund for Agricultural Development (IFAD), the United Nations Development Programme (UNDP), UNEP, the World Trade Organization (WTO) and the Consultative Group on International Agricultural Research (CGIAR).

** Such as: the International Treaty on Plant Genetic Resources for Food and Agriculture (ITPGRFA), the International Plant Protection Convention, the Convention on Biological Diversity (CBD), Codex Alimentarius, the United Nations Framework Convention on Climate Change (UNFCCC), the United Nations Convention to Combat Desertification and biodiversity related agreements.

There is no single blueprint for an ecosystem approach to crop production intensification. However, a range of farming practices and technologies, often location specific, have been developed. Chapters 2, 3, 4, 5 and 6 describe this rich toolkit of relevant, adoptable and adaptable ecosystem-based practices that enhance crop productivity and can serve as the cornerstone of national and regional programmes. Chapter 7 provides details of the policy environment and the institutional arrangements that will facilitate the adoption and implementation of SCPI on a large scale.

Chapter 2

Farming systems

Crop production intensification will be built on farming systems that offer a range of productivity, socio-economic and environmental benefits to producers and to society at large

Crops are grown under a wide range of production systems. At one end of the continuum is an interventionist approach, in which most aspects of production are controlled by technological interventions such as soil tilling, protective or curative pest and weed control with agrochemicals, and the application of mineral fertilizers for plant nutrition. At the other end are production systems that take a predominantly ecosystem approach and are both productive and more sustainable. These agro-ecological systems are generally characterized by minimal disturbance of the natural environment, plant nutrition from organic and non-organic sources, and the use of both natural and managed biodiversity to produce food, raw materials and other ecosystem services. Crop production based on an ecosystem approach sustains the health of farmland already in use, and can regenerate land left in poor condition by past misuse[1].

Farming systems for sustainable crop production intensification will offer a range of productivity, socio-economic and environmental benefits to producers and to society at large, including high and stable production and profitability; adaptation and reduced vulnerability to climate change; enhanced ecosystem functioning and services; and reductions in agriculture's greenhouse gas emissions and "carbon footprint".

These farming systems will be based on three technical principles:

- simultaneous achievement of increased agricultural productivity and enhancement of natural capital and ecosystem services;
- higher rates of efficiency in the use of key inputs, including water, nutrients, pesticides, energy, land and labour;
- use of managed and natural biodiversity to build system resilience to abiotic, biotic and economic stresses.

The farming practices required to implement those principles will differ according to local conditions and needs. However, in all cases they will need to:

- *minimize soil disturbance by minimizing mechanical tillage* in order to maintain soil organic matter, soil structure and overall soil health;
- *enhance and maintain a protective organic cover* on the soil surface, using crops, cover crops or crop residues, in order to protect the soil surface, conserve water and nutrients, promote

Contribution of sustainable intensification farming system practices to important ecosystem services

	System component			
Objective	**Mulch cover**	**Minimized or zero tillage**	**Legumes to supply plant nutrients**	**Crop rotation**
Simulate optimum "forest-floor" conditions	*	*		
Reduce evaporative loss of moisture from soil surface	*			
Reduce evaporative loss from upper soil layers	*	*		
Minimize oxidation of soil organic matter and loss of CO_2		*		
Minimize soil compaction	*	*		
Minimize temperature fluctuations at soil surface	*			
Provide regular supply of organic matter as substrate for soil organism activity	*			
Increase, maintain nitrogen levels in root zone	*	*	*	*
Increase cation exchange capacity of root zone	*	*	*	*
Maximize rain infiltration, minimize runoff	*	*		
Minimize soil loss in runoff and wind	*	*		
Permit, maintain natural layering of soil horizons through action of soil biota	*	*		
Minimize weeds	*	*		*
Increase rate of biomass production	*	*	*	*
Speed recuperation of soil porosity by soil biota	*	*	*	*
Reduce labour input		*		
Reduce fuel/energy inputs		*	*	*
Recycle nutrients	*	*	*	*
Reduce pest-pressure of pathogens				*
Rebuild damaged soil conditions and dynamics	*	*	*	*
Pollination services	*	*	*	*

Friedrich, T., Kassam, A.H. & Shaxson, F. 2009. Conservation agriculture. In: *Agriculture for developing countries. Science and technology options assessment (STOA) project.* European Parliament. Karlsruhe, Germany, European Technology Assessment Group.

soil biological activity and contribute to integrated weed and pest management;

- *cultivate a wider range of plant species* – both annuals and perennials – in associations, sequences and rotations that can include trees, shrubs, pastures and crops, in order to enhance crop nutrition and improve system resilience.

Those three key practices are generally associated with conservation agriculture (CA), which has been widely adopted in both developed and developing regions*. However, in order to achieve the sustainable intensification necessary for increased food production, they need to be supported by four additional management practices:

- *the use of well adapted, high-yielding varieties* with resistance to biotic and abiotic stresses and improved nutritional quality;
- *enhanced crop nutrition based on healthy soils*, through crop rotations and judicious use of organic and inorganic fertilizer;
- *integrated management of pests, diseases and weeds* using appropriate practices, biodiversity and selective, low risk pesticides when needed;
- *efficient water management*, by obtaining "more crops from fewer drops" while maintaining soil health and minimizing off-farm externalities.

Ideally, SCPI is the combination of all seven of those practices applied simultaneously in a timely and efficient manner. However, the very nature of sustainable production systems is dynamic: they should offer farmers many combinations of practices to choose from and adapt, according to their local production conditions and constraints[2-5].

Applied together, or in various combinations, the recommended practices contribute to important ecosystems services and work synergistically to produce positive outcomes in terms of factor and overall productivity. For example, for a given amount of rainfall, soil moisture availability to plants depends on how the soil surface, soil organic matter and plant root systems are managed. Water productivity under good soil moisture supply is enhanced when soils are healthy and plant nutrition is adequate. Good water infiltration and soil cover also minimize surface evaporation and maximize water

* Conservation agriculture is now practised on about 117 million ha worldwide, or about 8 percent of total crop land. Highest adoption levels (above 50 percent of crop land) are found in Australia, Canada and the southern cone of South America. Adoption is increasing in Africa, Central Asia and China.

use efficiency and productivity, in which the plants' own capacity to absorb and use water also plays a role.

One of the main requirements for ecologically sustainable production is healthy soil, creating an environment in the root zone that optimizes soil biota activity and permits root functioning to the maximum possible extent. Roots are able to capture plant nutrients and water and interact with a range of soil micro-organisms beneficial to soil health and crop performance[2, 6, 7]. Maintenance or improvement of soil organic matter content, soil structure and associated porosity are critical indicators of sustainable production and other ecosystem services.

To be sustainable in the long term, the loss of organic matter in any agricultural system must never exceed the rate of soil formation. In most agro-ecosystems, that is not possible if the soil is mechanically disturbed[8]. Therefore, a key starting point for sustainable production intensification – and a major building block of SCPI – is maintaining soil structure and organic matter content by limiting the use of mechanical soil disturbance in the process of crop establishment and subsequent crop management.

Minimized or zero tillage production methods – as practised in conservation agriculture – have significantly improved soil conditions, reduced degradation and enhanced productivity in many parts of the world. Most agricultural land continues to be ploughed, harrowed or hoed before every crop and during crop growth. The aim is to destroy weeds and facilitate water infiltration and crop establishment. However, recurring disturbance of topsoil buries soil cover and may destabilize soil structure. An additional effect is compaction of the soil, which reduces productivity[9].

One contribution of conservation agriculture to sustainable production intensification is minimizing soil disturbance and retaining the integrity of crop residues on the soil surface. CA approaches include minimized (or strip) tillage, which disturbs only the portion of the soil that is to contain the seed row, and zero tillage (also called no-tillage or direct seeding), in which mechanical disturbance of the soil is eliminated and crops are planted directly into a seedbed that has not been tilled since the previous crop[3].

Another management consideration relevant to SCPI is the role of farm power and mechanization. In many countries, the lack of farm power is a major constraint to intensification of production[10].

Using manual labour only, a farmer can grow enough food to feed, on average, three other people. With animal traction, the number doubles, and with a tractor increases to 50 or more[11]. Appropriate mechanization can lead to improved energy efficiency in crop production, which enhances sustainability and productive capacity and reduces harmful effects on the environment[12, 13].

At the same time, uncertainty about the price and availability of energy in the future suggests the need for measures to reduce overall requirements for farm power and energy. Conservation agriculture can lower those requirements by up to 60 percent, compared to conventional farming. The saving is due to the fact that most power intensive field operations, such as tillage, are eliminated or minimized, which eases labour and power bottlenecks particularly during land preparation. Investment in equipment, notably the number and size of tractors, is significantly reduced (although CA requires investment in new and appropriate farm implements). The savings also apply to small-scale farmers using hand labour or animal traction. Studies in the United Republic of Tanzania indicate that in the fourth year of implementing zero-tillage maize with cover crops, labour requirements fell by more than half[14].

Potential constraints

Some farming regions present special challenges to the introduction of specific SCPI practices. For example, under conservation agriculture, the lack of rainfall in subhumid and semi-arid climatic zones may limit production of biomass, which limits both the quantity of harvestable crops and the amount of residues available for use as soil cover, fodder or fuel. However, the water savings achieved by not tilling the soil generally lead to yield increases in the first years of adoption, despite the lack of residues. Scarcity of plant nutrients may prove to be a limiting factor in more humid areas, but the higher levels of soil biological activity achieved can enhance the long term availability of phosphorus and other nutrients[7, 15].

Low soil disturbance or zero tillage systems are often seen as unsuitable for farming on badly drained or compacted soils, or on heavy clay soils in cold and moist climates. In the first case, if bad drainage is caused by an impermeable soil horizon beyond the reach of tillage equipment, only biological means – such as tap roots, earthworms and termites – can break up such deep barriers to water percolation. Over time, these biological solutions are facilitated by minimal soil disturbance. In the second case, mulch-covered soils do take longer to warm up and dry, compared to ploughed land. However, zero tillage is practised successfully by farmers under very cold conditions in Canada and Finland, where studies have found that the temperature of covered soils does not fall as much in winter[13, 16].

Another misperception of minimized or zero tillage systems is that they increase the use of insecticides and herbicides. In some intensive systems, the integrated use of zero tillage, mulching and crop diversification has led to reductions in the use of insecticides and herbicides, in terms of both absolute amounts and active ingredient applied per tonne of output, compared with tillage-based agriculture[12, 13].

In manual smallholder systems, herbicides can be replaced by integrated weed management. For example, since conservation agriculture was introduced in 2005 in Karatu district, the United Republic of Tanzania, farmers have stopped ploughing and hoeing and are growing mixed crops of direct-seeded maize, hyacinth bean and pigeon pea. This system produces good surface mulch, so that weed management can be done by hand without need for herbicides. In some years, fields are rotated into wheat. The overall results have been positive, with average per hectare maize yields increasing from 1 tonne to 6 tonnes. This dramatic yield increase was achieved without agrochemicals and using livestock manure as a soil amendment and fertilizer[17].

Another potential bottleneck for wide adoption of conservation agriculture is the lack of suitable equipment, such as zero till seeders and planters, which are unavailable to small farmers in many developing countries. Even where this equipment is sold, it is often more expensive than conventional equipment and requires considerable initial investment. Such bottlenecks can be overcome by facilitating input supply chains and local manufacturing of equipment, and by promoting contractor services or equipment sharing schemes among farmers in order to reduce costs. Excellent examples of these approaches can be found on the Indo-Gangetic Plain. In most small farm scenarios, zero-till planters that use animal traction would meet and exceed the needs of a single farmer.

Farming systems that save and grow

An ecosystem approach to the intensification of crop production is most effective when the appropriate, mutually reinforcing practices are applied together. Even where it is not possible to implement all recommended practices at the same time, improvement towards that goal should be encouraged. The principles of SCPI can be readily integrated into farming systems that either have features in common with ecosystem-based approaches or can be improved by underpinning them with similar principles.

Integrated crop-livestock production

Integrated crop-livestock production systems are practised by most smallholders in developing countries. Pastureland has important ecological functions: it contains a high percentage of perennial grasses, which sequester and safely store large amounts of carbon in the soil at rates far exceeding those of annual crops. That capacity can be further enhanced with appropriate management – for example, by replacing exported nutrients, maintaining diversity in plant species, and allowing for sufficient recovery periods between use of land for grazing or cutting.

In conventional farming systems, there is a clear distinction between arable crops and pastureland. With SCPI, this distinction no longer exists, since annual crops may be rotated with pasture without the destructive intervention of soil tillage. This "pasture cropping" is an exciting development in a number of countries. In Australia, pasture cropping involves direct-drilling winter crops, such as oats, into predominantly summer-growing pastures of mainly native species. Benefits suggested by field experiments include reduced risk of waterlogging, nitrate leaching and soil erosion[18].

Practical innovations have harnessed synergies between crop, livestock and agroforestry production to enhance economic and ecological sustainability while providing a flow of valued ecosystem services. Through increased biological diversity, efficient nutrient recycling, improved soil health and forest conservation, these systems increase environmental resilience, and contribute to climate change adaptation and mitigation. They also enhance livelihood diversification and efficiency by optimizing production inputs, including labour, and increase resilience to economic stresses[19].

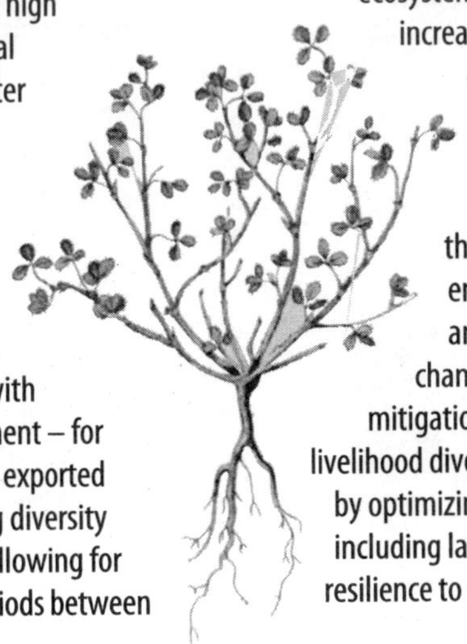

alfalfa

Sustainable rice-wheat production

Sustainable productivity in rice-wheat farming systems was pioneered on the Indo-Gangetic Plain of Bangladesh, India, Nepal and Pakistan by the Rice-Wheat Consortium, an initiative of the CGIAR and national agriculture research centres. It was launched in the 1990s in response to evidence of a plateau in crop productivity, loss of soil organic matter and receding groundwater tables[20].

wheat

The system involves the planting of wheat after rice using a tractor-drawn seed drill, which seeds directly into unploughed fields with a single pass. As this specialized agricultural machinery was originally not available in South Asia, the key to diffusion of the technology was creating a local manufacturing capacity to supply affordable zero tillage drills. An IFPRI study[21] found that zero tillage wheat provides immediate, identifiable and demonstrable economic benefits. It permits earlier planting, helps control weeds and has significant resource conservation benefits, including reduced use of diesel fuel and irrigation water. Cost savings are estimated at US$52 per hectare, primarily owing to a drastic reduction in tractor time and fuel for land preparation and wheat establishment.

Financial advantage of zero tillage over conventional tillage in Haryana, India (US$/ha)

Erenstein, O. 2009. *Adoption and impact of conservation agriculture based resource conserving technologies in South Asia. In:* Proceedings of the 4th world congress on conservation agriculture, February 4–7, 2009, New Delhi, India. *New Delhi, World Congress on Conservation Agriculture.*

Some 620 000 farmers on 1.8 million ha of the Indo-Gangetic Plain have adopted the system, with average income gains of US$180 to US$340 per household. Replicating the approach elsewhere will require on-farm adaptive and participatory research and development, links between farmers and technology suppliers and, above all, interventions that are financially attractive.

tagasaste

Agroforestry

Agroforestry systems, involving the cultivation of woody perennials and annual crops, are increasingly practised on degraded land, usually with perennial legumes. Conservation agriculture works well with agroforestry and several tree crop systems, and farmers in both developing and developed regions practise it in some form. These systems could be further enhanced by improved crop associations, including legumes, and integration with livestock. Alley cropping is one innovation in this area that offers productivity, economic and environmental benefits to producers[22]. Another example is the use of varying densities of "fertilizer trees" that enhance biological nitrogen fixation, conserve moisture and increase production of biomass for use as surface residues (see Chapter 3, ***Soil health***).

Ripper-furrower system in Namibia

Farmers in the north of Namibia are using conservation agriculture practices to grow drought tolerant crops, including millet, sorghum and maize. The farming system uses a tractor-drawn ripper-furrower to rip the hard pan to a depth of 60 cm and form furrows for in-field rainfall harvesting. The harvested water is concentrated in the root zone of crops, which are planted in the rip lines together with a mixture of fertilizer and manure. Tractors are used in the first year to establish the system. From the second year, farmers plant crops directly into the rip lines using an animal-drawn direct seeder.

Crop residues are consumed mainly by livestock, but the increased biomass produced by the system also provides some residues for soil cover. Farmers are encouraged to practise crop rotation with legumes. Those techniques lengthen the growing season and improve soil structure, fertility and moisture retention. Average maize yields have increased from 300 kg/ha to more than 1.5 tonnes.

Other production systems

Organic farming, when practised in combination with conservation agriculture, can lead to improved soil health and productivity, increased efficiency in the use of organic matter and energy savings. Organic CA farming serves mainly niche markets and is practised in parts of Brazil, Germany and the United States of America, and by some subsistence farmers in Africa.

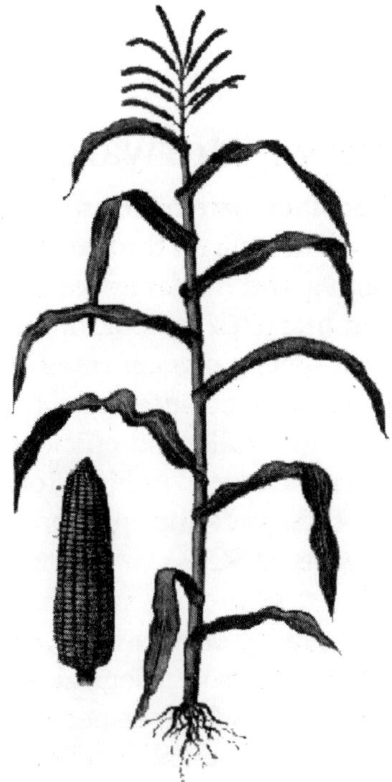

maize

Shifting cultivation entails the clearing for crop production of forest land that is subsequently abandoned, allowing natural reforestation and the recovery of depleted plant nutrients. Although shifting cultivation is often viewed negatively, it can be adapted to follow SCPI principles. In place of slash-and-burn, shifting cultivators could adopt slash-and-mulch systems, in which diversified cropping (including legumes and perennials) reduces the need for land clearing. Other ecosystem-based approaches, such as the ***System of Rice Intensification***, have also proven, in specific circumstances, to be successful as a basis for sustainable intensification[23].

The way forward

Farming systems for sustainable crop production intensification will be built on the three core technical principles outlined in this chapter, and implemented using the seven recommended management practices: minimum soil disturbance, permanent organic soil cover, species diversification, use of high-yielding adapted varieties from good seed, integrated pest management, plant nutrition based on healthy soils, and efficient water management. The integration of pastures, trees and livestock into the production system, and the use of adequate and appropriate farm power and equipment, are also key parts of SCPI.

The shift to SCPI systems can occur rapidly when there is a suitable enabling environment, or gradually in areas where farmers face particular agro-ecological, socio-economic or policy constraints, including a lack of the necessary equipment. While some economic and environmental benefits will be achieved in the short term, a longer term commitment from all stakeholders is necessary in order to achieve the full benefits of such systems.

Monitoring of progress in production system practices and their outcomes will be essential. Relevant socio-economic indicators include farm profit, factor productivity, the amount of external inputs applied per unit of output, the number of farmers practising sustainable intensified systems, the area covered, and the stability of production. Relevant ecosystem service indicators are: satisfactory levels of soil organic matter, clean water provisioning from an intensive agriculture area, reduced erosion, increased biodiversity and wildlife within agricultural landscapes, and reductions in both carbon footprint and greenhouse gas emissions.

Production systems for SCPI are knowledge-intensive and relatively complex to learn and implement. For most farmers, extensionists, researchers and policymakers, they are a new way of doing business. Consequently, there is an urgent need to build capacity and provide learning opportunities (for example, through farmer field schools) and technical support in order to improve the skills all stakeholders. That will require coordinated support at the international and regional levels to strengthen national and local institutions. Formal education and training at tertiary and secondary levels will need to upgrade their curricula to include the teaching of SCPI principles and practices.

Chapter 3

Soil health

Agriculture must, literally, return to its roots by rediscovering the importance of healthy soil, drawing on natural sources of plant nutrition, and using mineral fertilizer wisely

Soil is fundamental to crop production. Without soil, no food could be produced on a large scale, nor would livestock be fed. Because it is finite and fragile, soil is a precious resource that requires special care from its users. Many of today's soil and crop management systems are unsustainable. At one extreme, overuse of fertilizer has led, in the European Union, to nitrogen (N) deposition that threatens the sustainability of an estimated 70 percent of nature[1]. At the other extreme, in most parts of sub-Saharan Africa, the under-use of fertilizer means that soil nutrients exported with crops are not being replenished, leading to soil degradation and declining yields.

How did the current situation arise? The main driver was the quadrupling of world population over the past 100 years, which demanded a fundamental change in soil and crop management in order to produce more food. That was achieved thanks partly to the development and massive use of mineral fertilizers, especially of nitrogen, since N availability is the most important determinant of yield in all major crops[2-5].

Before the discovery of mineral N fertilizers, it took centuries to build up nitrogen stocks in the soil[6]. By contrast, the explosion in food production in Asia during the Green Revolution was due largely to the intensive use of mineral fertilization, along with improved germplasm and irrigation. World production of mineral fertilizers increased almost 350 percent between 1961 and 2002, from 33 million tonnes to 146 million tonnes[7]. Over the past 40 years, mineral fertilizers accounted for an estimated 40 percent of the increase in food production[8].

The contribution of fertilizers to food production has also carried significant costs to the environment. Today, Asia and Europe have the world's highest rates of mineral fertilizer use per hectare. They also face the greatest problems of environmental pollution resulting from excessive fertilizer use, including soil and water acidification, contamination of surface and groundwater resources, and increased emissions of potent greenhouse gases. The N-uptake efficiency in China is only about 26-28 percent for rice, wheat and maize and less than 20 percent for vegetable crops[9]. The remainder is simply lost to the environment.

The impact of mineral fertilizers on the environment is a question of management – for example, how much is applied compared to the amount exported with crops, or the method and timing of applications. In other words, it is the *efficiency* of fertilizer use, especially of N and phosphorus (P), which determines if this aspect of soil management is a boon for crops, or a negative for the environment.

The challenge, therefore, is to abandon current unsustainable practices and move to land husbandry that can provide a sound foundation for sustainable crop production intensification. Far-reaching changes in soil management are called for in many countries. The new approaches advocated here build on work undertaken by both FAO[10-12] and many other institutions[13-20], and focus on the management of soil health.

Principles of soil health management

Soil health has been defined as: "the capacity of soil to function as a living system. Healthy soils maintain a diverse community of soil organisms that help to control plant disease, insect and weed pests, form beneficial symbiotic associations with plant roots, recycle essential plant nutrients, improve soil structure with positive repercussions for soil water and nutrient holding capacity, and ultimately improve crop production"[21]. To that definition, an ecosystem perspective can be added: A healthy soil does not pollute the environment; rather, it contributes to mitigating climate change by maintaining or increasing its carbon content.

Soil contains one of the Earth's most diverse assemblages of living organisms, intimately linked via a complex food web. It can be either sick or healthy, depending on how it is managed. Two crucial characteristics of a healthy soil are the rich diversity of its biota and the high content of non-living soil organic matter. If the organic matter is increased or maintained at a satisfactory level for productive crop growth, it can be reasonably assumed that a soil is healthy. Healthy soil is resilient to outbreaks of soil-borne pests. For example, the parasitic weed, *Striga*, is far less of a problem in healthy soils[22]. Even the damage caused by pests not found in the soil, such as maize stem borers, is reduced in fertile soils[23].

The diversity of soil biota is greater in the tropics than in temperate zones[24]. Because the rate of agricultural intensification in the future will generally be greater in the tropics, agro-ecosystems there are under particular threat of soil degradation. Any losses of biodiversity and, ultimately, ecosystem functioning, will affect subsistence farmers in the tropics more than in other regions, because they rely to a larger extent on these processes and their services.

Functional interactions of soil biota with organic and inorganic components, air and water determine a soil's potential to store and release nutrients and water to plants, and to promote and sustain plant growth. Large reserves of stored nutrients are, in themselves, no guarantee of high soil fertility or high crop production. As plants take up most of their nutrients in a water soluble form, nutrient transformation and cycling – through processes that may be biological, chemical or physical in nature – are essential. The nutrients need to be transported to plant roots through free-flowing water. Soil structure is, therefore, another key component of a healthy soil because it determines a soil's water-holding capacity and rooting depth. The rooting depth may be restricted by physical constraints, such as a high water table, bedrock or other impenetrable layers, as well as by chemical problems such as soil acidity, salinity, sodality or toxic substances.

A shortage of any one of the 15 nutrients required for plant growth can limit crop yield. To achieve the higher productivity needed to meet current and future food demand, it is imperative to ensure their availability in soils and to apply a balanced amount of nutrients from organic sources and from mineral fertilizers, if required. The timely provision of micronutrients in "fortified" fertilizers is a potential source of enhanced crop nutrition where deficiencies occur.

Nitrogen can also be added to soil by integrating N-fixing legumes and trees into cropping systems (see also Chapter 2, *Farming systems*). Because they have deep roots, trees and some soil-improving legumes have the capacity to pump up from the subsoil nutrients that would otherwise never reach crops. Crop nutrition can be enhanced by other biological associations – for example, between crop roots and soil mycorrhizae, which help cassava to capture phosphorus in depleted soils. Where these ecosystem processes fail to supply sufficient nutrients for high yields, intensive production will depend on the judicious and efficient application of mineral fertilizers.

A combination of ecosystem processes and wise use of mineral fertilizers forms the basis of a sustainable soil health management system that has the capacity to produce higher yields while using fewer external inputs.

Technologies that save and grow

No single technology is likely to address the specific soil health and soil fertility constraints that prevail in different locations. However, the basic principles of good soil health management, outlined above, have been successfully applied in a wide range of agro-ecologies and under diverse socio-economic conditions.

Building on soil health management principles, research in different regions of the world has identified some "best-bet" technologies. The following examples describe crop management systems that have high potential for intensification and sustainable production. They address specific soil fertility problems in different agro-ecological zones and have been widely adopted by farmers. They may serve as templates for national partners in devising policies that encourage farmers to adopt these technologies as part of sustainable intensification.

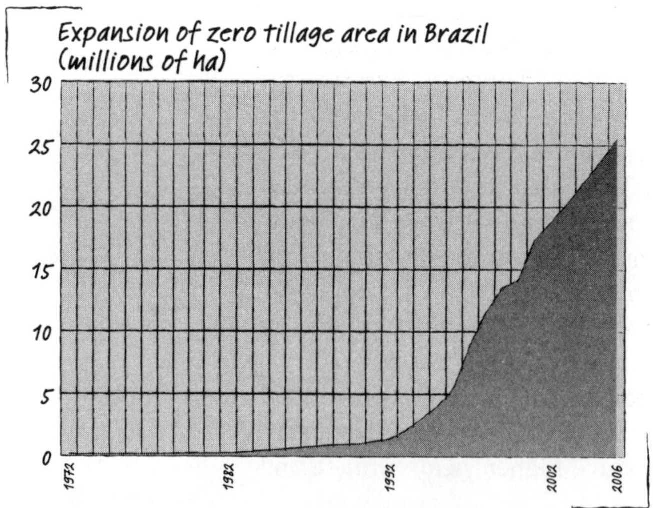

de Moraes Sá, J.C. 2010. No-till cropping system in Brazil: Its perspectives and new technologies to improve and develop. *Presentation prepared for the International Conference on Agricultural Engineering, 6-8 September 2010, Clermont-Ferrand, France (http://www.ageng2010.com/files/file-inline/J-C-M-SA.pdf).*

Increasing soil organic matter in soils in Latin America

Oxisols and ultisols are the dominant soil types in Brazil's Cerrado tropical savanna and Amazon rainforest regions, and they are also widespread in Africa's humid forest zone. Among the oldest on earth, these soils are poor in nutrients and very acidic, owing to their low capacity to hold nutrients – and cations in particular – in their surface and subsoil layers. In addition, being located in regions with high rainfall, they are prone to erosion if the surface is not protected by vegetative cover.

Upon conversion of the land from natural vegetation to agricultural use, special care has to be taken to minimize losses of soil organic matter. Management systems for these soils have been designed to conserve or even increase organic matter by providing permanent soil cover, using a mulching material rich in carbon, and ensuring minimized or zero tillage of the soil surface. These practices are all key components of the SCPI approach.

Such systems are being rapidly adopted by farmers in many parts of Latin America, and particularly in humid and subhumid zones, because they control soil erosion and generate savings by reducing labour inputs. Adoption has been facilitated by close collaboration between government research and extension services, farmer associations and private companies that produce agrochemicals, seed and machinery. Zero-till farming has spread rapidly and now covers 26 million hectares on oxisols and ultisols in Brazil.

Biological nitrogen fixation to enrich N-poor soils in African savannas

Crop production in the savanna regions of western, eastern and southern Africa is severely constrained by N- and P-deficiency in soils[17, 25], as well as the lack of micronutrients such as zinc and molybdenum. The use of leguminous crops and trees that are able to fix atmospheric nitrogen, in combination with applications of mineral P-fertilizers, has shown very promising results in on-farm evaluations conducted by the Tropical Soil Biology and Fertility Institute, the World Agroforestry Centre and the International Institute of Tropical Agriculture (IITA).

The combination of mineral fertilizer application and a dual-purpose grain legume, such as soybean, intercropped or relay-cropped with maize, increased maize yields in Kenya by 140 to 300 percent[17] and resulted in a positive N-balance in the cropping system. Dual-purpose grain legumes produce a large amount of biomass with their haulms and roots, as well as an acceptable grain yield. Several farming communities in eastern and southern Africa have adopted this system[26]. It has the additional advantage of helping farmers to combat *Striga* – some soybean cultivars act as "trap crops", which force *Striga* seeds to germinate when the weed's usual hosts, maize or sorghum, are not present[10, 27].

In eastern and southern Africa, N-deficient maize cropping systems have become more productive thanks to improved fallows using leguminous trees and shrubs. Per hectare, species such as *Sesbania sesban*, *Tephrosia vogelii* and *Crotalaria ochroleuca* accumulate in their leaves and roots around 100 to 200 kg of nitrogen – two-thirds of it from nitrogen fixation – over a period of six months to two years. Along with subsequent applications of mineral fertilizer, these improved fallows provide sufficient N for up to three subsequent maize crops, resulting in yields as much as four times higher than those obtained in non-fallow systems.

Research indicates that a full agroforestry system with crop-fallow rotations and high value trees can triple a farm's carbon stocks in 20 years[28]. The system has been so successful that tens of thousands of farmers in Kenya, Malawi, Mozambique, Uganda, the United Republic of Tanzania, Zambia and Zimbabwe are now adapting the component technologies to their local conditions.

Sesbania sesban

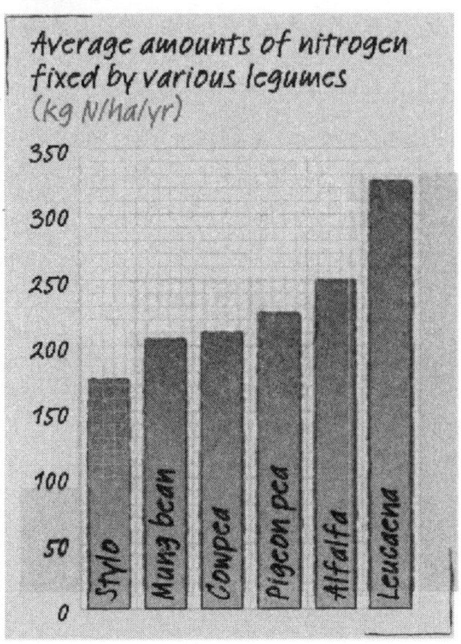

FAO. 1984. Legume inoculants and their use. *Rome.*

Faidherbia albida

Evergreen agriculture in Africa's Sahel

The African acacia, *Faidherbia albida*, is a natural component of farming systems in the Sahel. It is highly compatible with food crops because it does not compete with them for light, nutrients or water. In fact, the tree loses its nitrogen-rich leaves during the rainy season, thus providing a protective mulch which also serves as natural fertilizer for crops. Zambia's Conservation Farming Unit has reported unfertilized maize yields of 4.1 tonnes per hectare in the vicinity of *Faidherbia* trees, compared to 1.3 tonnes from maize grown nearby, but outside of the tree canopy[29]. Today, more than 160 000 farmers in Zambia are growing food crops on 300 000 ha with *Faidherbia*. Similarly promising results have been observed in Malawi, where maize yields near *Faidherbia* trees are almost three times higher than yields outside their range. In Niger, there are now more than 4.8 million hectares under *Faidherbia*-based agroforesty, resulting in enhanced millet and sorghum production.

Thousands of rainfed smallholdings in Burkina Faso are also shifting to these "evergreen" farming systems.

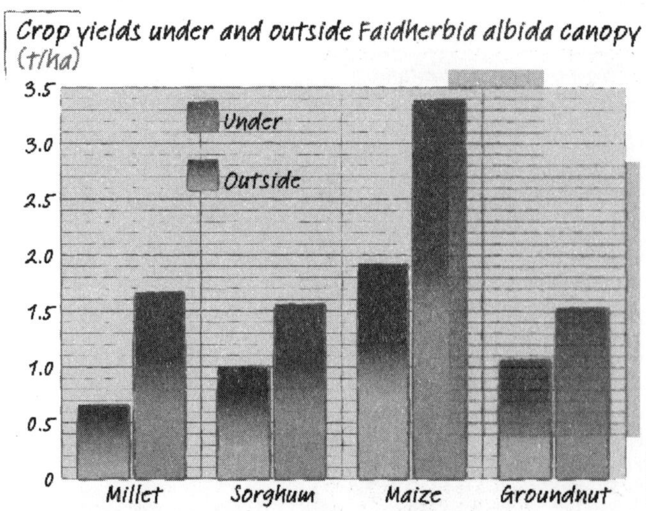

FAO. 1999. Agroforestry parklands in sub-Saharan Africa, by J.-M. Boffa. Rome.

"Urea deep placement" for rice in Bangladesh

Throughout Asia, farmers apply nitrogen fertilizer to rice before transplanting by broadcasting a basal application of urea onto wet soil, or into standing water, and then broadcasting one or more top-dressings of urea in the weeks after transplanting up to the flowering stage. Such practices are agronomically and economically inefficient and environmentally harmful. The rice plants use only about a third of the fertilizer applied[30], while much of the remainder is lost to the air through volatilization and surface water run-off. Only a small amount remains in the soil and is available to subsequent crops.

One way of reducing N losses is to compress prilled urea to form urea super granules (USG) which are inserted 7 to 10 cm deep in the soil between plants. This "urea deep placement" (UDP) doubles the percentage of nitrogen taken up by plants[31-35], reduces N lost to the air and to

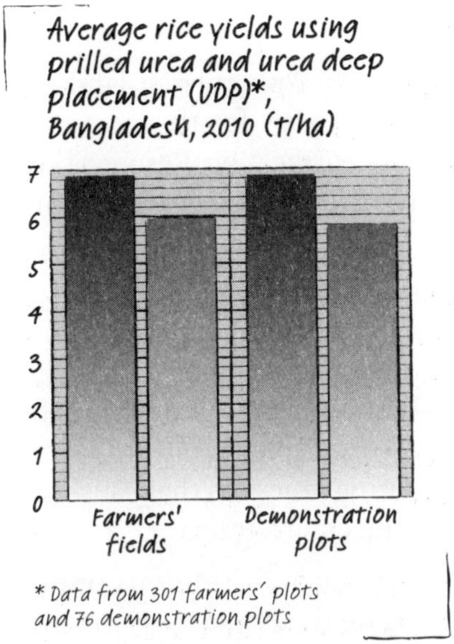

IFDC. 2010. Improved livelihood for Sidr-affected rice farmers (ILSAFARM). *Quarterly report submitted to USAID-Bangladesh, No. 388-A-00-09-00004-00. Muscle Shoals, USA.*

surface water run-off, and has produced average yield increases of 18 percent in farmers' fields. The International Fertilizer Development Center and the United States Agency for International Development are helping smallholder farmers to upscale UDP technology throughout Bangladesh. The goal is to reach two million farmers in five years[36]. The technology is spreading fast in Bangladesh and is being investigated by 15 other countries, most of them in sub-Saharan Africa. The machines used to produce USG in Bangladesh are manufactured locally and cost between US$1 500 and US$2 000.

Site-specific nutrient management in intensive rice

The International Rice Research Institute (IRRI) and its national partners have developed the site-specific nutrient management (SSNM) system for highly intensive rice production. SSNM is a sophisticated knowledge system focused on double and triple rice mono-cropping. Tests at 180 sites in eight key irrigated rice domains of Asia found that the system led to a 30 to 40 percent increase in N-use efficiency, mainly thanks to improved N management. Across all sites and four successive rice crops, profitability increased by an average of 12 percent.

In several provinces of China, SSNM reduced farmers' use of N-fertilizer by one third, while increasing yields by 5 percent[37]. A site-specific N-management strategy was able to increase uptake efficiency by almost 370 percent on the North China Plain[9]. Since the average plant recovery efficiency of nitrogen fertilizer in intensive rice systems is only about 30 percent, those are remarkable achievements that contribute substantially to reducing the negative environmental effects of rice production. The complex SSNM technology is being simplified in order to facilitate its wider adoption by farmers.

rice

The way forward

The following actions are required to improve current land husbandry practices and provide a sound basis for the successful adoption of sustainable crop production intensification. Responsibility for implementation rests with national partners, assisted by FAO and other international agencies.

Establish national regulations for sound land husbandry. A supportive policy framework should aim at encouraging farmers to adopt sustainable farming systems based on healthy soils. Leadership is required to establish and monitor best practices, with the active participation of smallholder farmers and their communities. Governments must be prepared to regulate farming practices that cause soil degradation or pose serious threats to the environment.

Monitor soil health. Policymakers and national institutions responsible for the environment are demanding methods and tools to verify the impact of farming practices. While monitoring soil health is a very challenging task, efforts are under way to implement it at global[38], regional and national scales[39]. Monitoring the impact of agricultural production has advanced in developed countries, but is just beginning in many developing countries. FAO and its partners have developed a list of methods and tools for undertaking assessments and monitoring tasks[40]. Core land quality indicators requiring immediate and longer term development should be distinguished[41]. Priority indicators are soil organic matter content, nutrient balance, yield gap, land use intensity and diversity, and land cover. Indicators that still need to be developed are soil quality, land degradation and agrobiodiversity.

Build capacity. Soil health management is knowledge-intensive and its wide adoption will require capacity building through training programmes for extension workers and farmers. The skills of researchers will also need to be upgraded at both national and international levels, in order to provide the enhanced knowledge necessary to support soil management under SCPI. Policymakers should explore new approaches, such as support groups for adaptive research cooperation[42], which provide technical support and on-the-job training for national research institutions and translate research results into practical guidelines for small farmers. National capacity to undertake on-farm research must also be strengthened, and focused on addressing spatial and temporal variability through, for example, better use of ecosystems modelling.

Disseminate information and communicate benefits. Any large-scale implementation of soil health management requires that supporting information is made widely available, particularly through channels familiar to farmers and extension workers. Given the very high priority attached to soil health in SCPI, media outlets should include not only national newspapers and radio programmes, but also modern information and communication technologies, such as cellular phones and the Internet, which can be much more effective in reaching younger farmers.

Chapter 4

Crops and varieties

Farmers will need a genetically diverse portfolio of improved crop varieties, suited to a range of agro-ecosystems and farming practices, and resilient to climate change

Sustainable crop production intensification will use crops and varieties that are better adapted to ecologically based production practices than those currently available, which were bred for high-input agriculture. The targeted use of external inputs will require plants that are more productive, use nutrients and water more efficiently, have greater resistance to insect pests and diseases, and are more tolerant to drought, flood, frost and higher temperatures. SCPI varieties will need to be adapted to less favoured areas and production systems, produce food with higher nutritional value and desirable organoleptic properties, and help improve the provision of ecosystem services.

Those new crops and varieties will be deployed in increasingly diverse production systems where associated agricultural biodiversity – such as livestock, pollinators, predators of pests, soil organisms and nitrogen fixing trees – is also important. Varieties suitable for SCPI will need to be adapted to changing production practices and farming systems (see Chapter 2) and to integrated pest management (see Chapter 6).

SCPI will be undertaken in combination with adaptation to climate change, which is expected to lead to alterations in timing, frequency and amounts of rainfall, with serious droughts in some areas and floods in others. Increased occurrence of extreme weather events is probable, along with soil erosion, land degradation and loss of biodiversity. Many of the characteristics required for adaptation to climate change are similar to those needed for SCPI. Increased genetic diversity will improve adaptability, while greater resistance to biotic and abiotic stresses will improve cropping system resilience.

Achieving SCPI means developing not only a new range of varieties, but also an increasingly diverse portfolio of varieties of an extended range of crops, many of which currently receive little attention from public or private plant breeders. Farmers will also need the means and opportunity to deploy these materials in their different production systems. That is why the management of plant genetic resources (PGR), development of crops and varieties, and the delivery of appropriate, high quality seeds and planting materials to farmers are fundamental contributions to SCPI.

Principles, concepts and constraints

The system that will provide high-yielding and adapted varieties to farmers has three parts: *PGR conservation and distribution*, *variety development* and *seed production and delivery*. The stronger the links among these different parts, the better the whole system will function. Conserved and improved materials will need to be available for variety development, and new varieties will have to be generated at a pace that meets changing demands and requirements. Timely delivery to farmers of suitably adapted materials, of the right quality and quantity, at an acceptable cost, is essential. To work well, the system needs an appropriate institutional framework, as well as policies and practices that support its component parts and the links between them.

The improved conservation of PGR – *ex situ*, *in situ* and on-farm – and the enhanced delivery of germplasm to different users depend on coordinated efforts at international, national and local levels[1]. Today genebanks around the world conserve some 7.4 million accessions. These are complemented by the *in situ* conservation of traditional varieties and crop wild relatives by national programmes and farmers, and by the materials maintained in public and private sector breeding programmes[2]. Strong national conservation programmes, combined with the improved availability and increased distribution of a wider range of inter- and intra-specific diversity, will be critical to successful implementation of SCPI.

Technical, policy and institutional issues influence the effectiveness of programmes for crop improvement. A wide range of diverse materials is needed for the pre-breeding of varieties. Molecular genetics and other biotechnologies are now widely used by both national and private sector breeding programmes and can make an essential contribution to meeting SCPI breeding objectives[3]. The policy and regulatory dimension needs to include not only variety release, but also provisions for intellectual property protection, seed laws and the use of restriction technologies.

The benefits of PGR conservation and plant breeding will not be realized unless quality seeds of improved varieties reach farmers through an effective seed multiplication and delivery system. Variety testing of promising materials from breeding programmes needs to be followed by the prompt release of the best varieties for early generation seed multiplication. Certified seed production, along with quality assurance provided by the national seed service, are essential next steps before seed is sold to farmers. Both the public and private sectors should support this value chain and, where possible, local seed enterprises should produce certified seed and market it to farmers.

Smallholder farmers around the world still rely heavily on farmer-saved seed and have little access to commercial seed systems. In some countries, well over 70 percent of seed, even of major crops, is managed within the farmer seed system. Both formal and saved seed systems will be essential in the distribution of SCPI-adapted materials. The various practices and procedures adopted to support SCPI will need to take account of how farmer seed systems operate, and strengthen them in order to increase the supply of new materials.

Ensuring that the different parts of the PGR and seed supply system are able to meet the challenges of SCPI requires an effective policy and regulatory framework, appropriate institutions, a continuing programme of capacity development and, above all, farmer participation. A strong programme of research, aimed at providing information, new techniques and materials, is also important. Ideally, the programme will reflect farmers' knowledge and experience, strengthen the linkages between farmers and research workers from different areas, and serve dynamic and changing needs.

Approaches that save and grow

Improving the conservation and use of plant genetic resources

Plant genetic resources – the inter- and intra-specific diversity of crops, varieties and related wild species – are central to agricultural development and improvements in both the quantity and quality of food and other agricultural products. Genes from traditional varieties and crop wild relatives were at the heart of the Green Revolution, providing the semi-dwarfing characters of modern wheat and rice varieties, as well as crop resistance to major insect pests and diseases.

The success of SCPI will depend on the use of PGR in new and better ways. However, the crucial importance of genes from local varieties and crop wild relatives in development of new varieties is matched by rising concern over the loss of diversity worldwide, and the need for its effective conservation. International recognition of PGR is reflected in the conclusions of the World Summit on Food Security[4], held in 2009, the ratification by more than 120 countries of the International Treaty on Plant Genetic Resources for Food and Agriculture (ITPGRFA)[5], and the strategic goals of the Convention on Biological Diversity (CBD)[6].

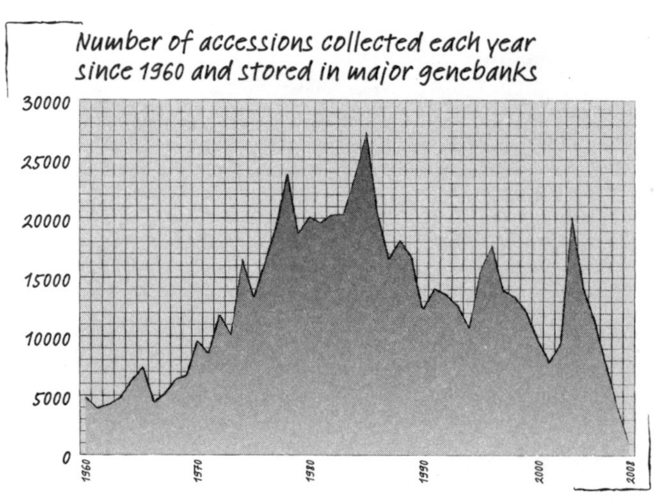

In mobilizing plant genetic resources for sustainable intensification, the international dimension will play a fundamental role. The international framework for conservation and sustainable use of PGR has been greatly strengthened by the International Treaty, the Global Crop Diversity Trust and the programme of work on agricultural biodiversity of the CBD. A global system that can provide support for SCPI is emerging. Since much of the diversity that will be needed may be conserved in other countries, or in the international genebanks of the CGIAR, national participation in international programmes will be indispensable.

Developing countries need to strengthen their national PGR programmes by enacting legislation to implement fully the provisions of the ITPGRFA. Guidelines on implementation have been prepared[7] and the Treaty Secretariat, Bioversity International and FAO are working on implementation issues in collaboration with some 15 countries. Implementing the revised Global Plan of Action on Plant Genetic Resources for Food and Agriculture and Article 9 of the ITPGRFA on Farmers' Rights will make an important contribution to the creation of the national operating

FAO. 2010. The Second Report on the State of the World's Plant Genetic Resources for Food and Agriculture. *Rome.*

framework for implementing sustainable intensification.

In order to adopt sustainable intensification strategies, countries will need to know the extent and distribution of the diversity of crop species and their wild relatives. Technologies for mapping diversity and locating diversity threatened by climate change have improved[8]. A major project supported by the Global Environment Facility in Armenia, Bolivia, Madagascar, Sri Lanka and Uzbekistan has established and tested ways of improving the conservation and use of crop wild relatives. The project developed and implemented area and species conservation management plans, identified climate change management actions to conserve useful diversity, and initiated plant breeding programmes using new materials identified thanks to the conservation and prioritization work[9].

Intensification will require an increased flow into breeding programmes of germplasm and promising varieties. The multilateral system of access and benefit sharing under the ITPGRFA provides the necessary international framework, although – given the increased importance of diversity to SCPI – it may need to be extended to a greater number of crops than those currently covered in Annex 1 of the Treaty. On the technical side, a number of procedures are available to identify useful materials in large collections, such as the Focused Identification of Germplasm Strategy now under development[10].

wild wheat

banana

Moving genetic material will also require improvements in the phytosanitary capacity and practices, as well as the distribution capacities, of genebanks.

The comprehensive characterization and evaluation of genebank collections at national and local levels, with farmers participating in the evaluation of potentially useful material, will make a key contribution to improving the use of PGR. Effective use also requires strong research and pre-breeding programmes. The Global Initiative on Plant Breeding is preparing a manual on pre-breeding to help develop that capacity. Ultimately, however, countries and the private breeding sector will need to support the strengthening of national agricultural research capacity, with the introduction of university courses on conservation and plant breeding for sustainable intensification.

Developing improved and adapted varieties

Sustainable intensification requires crop varieties that are suited to different agronomic practices, to farmers' needs in locally diverse agro-ecosystems and to the effects of climate change. Important traits will include greater tolerance to heat, drought and frost, increased input-use efficiency, and enhanced pest and disease resistance. It will involve the development of a larger number of varieties drawn from a greater diversity of breeding material.

Because new varieties take many years to produce, breeding programmes need to be stable, competently staffed and adequately funded. Both the public sector and private breeding companies will play an important part in developing those varieties, with the public sector often focusing on major staple crops, while the private sector would be concerned more with cash crops. The more open and vigorous the system, the more likely it is that the required new materials will be generated.

An important step forward will be a significant increase in public support to pre-breeding and breeding research. SCPI requires new materials, a redefinition of breeding objectives and practices, and the adoption of population breeding approaches. Properties such as production resilience and stability will need to be inherent, and not dependent on external inputs.

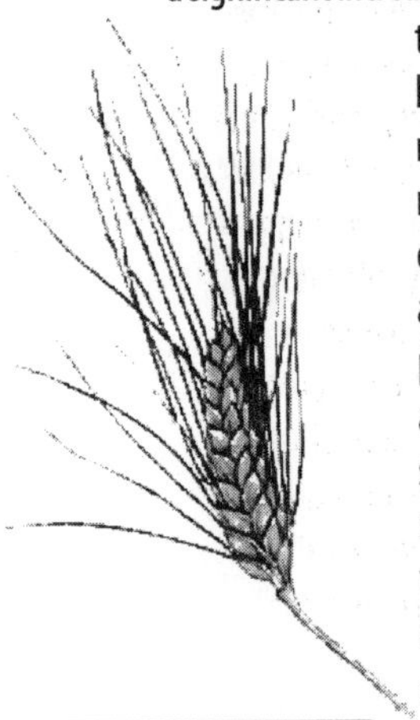

barley

It is unlikely that traditional public or private breeding programmes will be able to provide all the new plant material needed or produce the most appropriate varieties, especially of minor crops which command limited resources. Participatory plant breeding can help fill this gap.

For example, the International Centre for Agricultural Research in the Dry Areas (ICARDA), together with the Syrian Arab Republic and other Middle East and North African countries, has undertaken a programme for participatory breeding of barley which maintains high levels of diversity and produces improved material capable of good yields in conditions of very limited rainfall (less than 300 mm per year). Farmers participate in the selection of parent materials and in on-farm evaluations. In Syria, the procedure has produced significant barley yield improvements and increased the resistance of the barley varieties to drought stress[11].

Policies and regulations are needed to support the production of new varieties and ensure adequate returns to both public and private sector plant breeding. However, they may need to be more open and flexible than current patent-based procedures or arrangements under the International Union for the Protection of New Varieties of Plants (UPOV). The uniformity and stability properties of varieties adapted to SCPI may be different from those currently envisaged under UPOV, and Farmers' Rights, as identified in the ITPGRFA, need to be recognized. Most of all, policies and regulations must support the rapid release of SCPI adapted materials; in many countries far too much time is spent on the approval stage for new varieties.

The institutional framework that supports variety development and release is weak in a number of countries. University and other training programmes will need to be adjusted to furnish a greater number of plant breeders and breeding researchers trained in using crop improvement practices for SCPI. Farmers should be involved more fully both in the identification of breeding objectives and in the selection process. Extension services will need to be strengthened in order to respond to farmers' expressed needs and to provide sound practical guidance on the cultivation of new varieties.

Improving seed production and distribution

A key issue when planning SCPI programmes is to determine the status of the national seed system and its capacity to improve the provision of high quality seed of adapted varieties to farmers. An initial step should be the development, in consultation with all key stakeholders, of an appropriate seed policy and regulations for variety release.

The policy should provide a framework for better coordination of the public and private sectors, as well as an action plan for development of a seed industry that is capable of meeting farmers' needs for high quality seed. In many developing countries, the policy will also need to recognize farmer-saved seed as a major source of propagation material. Since local seed enterprises will play an important role in SCPI, creating an enabling environment for them is essential. The action plan should identify gaps and weaknesses in the sector and the main measures that are needed to resolve them.

An improved framework may also be needed for seed production and movement. Because regulations and legislation should favour the rapid deployment of new planting material, and the transfer of new varieties from one area to another, harmonization of legislation among countries is important. For example, 12 member countries of the Economic Community of West African States have adopted harmonized seed laws. The maintenance and use of a larger number of varieties may strain seed quality management systems; therefore, the development of a quality-declared seed system will help ensure that, in the process of adapting seed practices to sustainable intensification, quality does not suffer.

One likely consequence of sustainable intensification will be the increased importance of local seed producers and local markets in supplying farmers. The role of markets in maintaining diversity is increasingly recognized[12]. Markets can be supported through initiatives such as local diversity fairs, local seed banks and community biodiversity registers, which encourage the maintenance and distribution of local materials and favour improvements in their quality[8].

beans

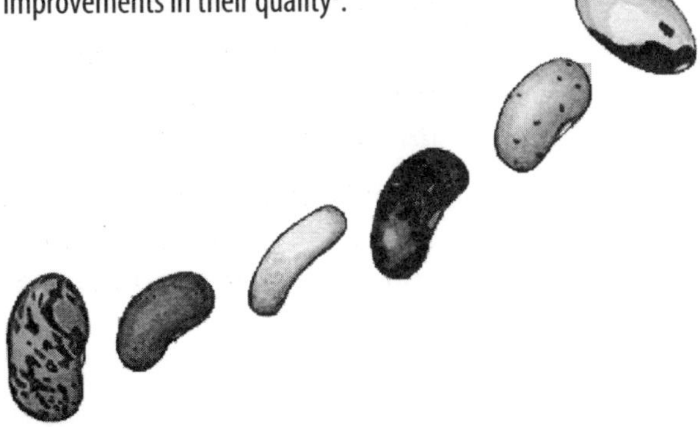

The way forward

Actions in the technical, policy and institutional arenas can help ensure that plant genetic resources and seed delivery systems function effectively to support sustainable crop production intensification. Although they will involve diverse institutions and take place at various scales, the required actions will have their greatest impact if they are coordinated. Recommended measures include:

- *Strengthening linkages between the conservation of PGR and the use of diversity in plant breeding*, particularly through improved characterization and evaluation of traits relevant to SCPI in a wider range of crops, increased support for pre-breeding and population improvement, and much closer collaboration among institutions concerned with conservation and breeding.
- *Increasing the participation of farmers in conservation, crop improvement and seed supply* in order to support work on a wider diversity of materials, to ensure that new varieties are appropriate to farmer practices and experiences, and to strengthen on-farm conservation of PGR and farmer seed supply systems.
- *Improving policies and legislation for variety development and release, and seed supply*, including national implementation of the provisions of the ITPGRFA, enactment of flexible variety release legislation, and the development or revision of seed policies and seed legislation.
- *Strengthening capacity* by creating a new generation of skilled practitioners to support enhanced breeding, work with farmers and explore the ways in which crops and varieties contribute to successful intensification.
- *Revitalizing the public sector and expanding its role* in developing new crop varieties, by creating an enabling environment for seed sector development and ensuring that farmers have the knowledge needed to deploy new materials.
- *Supporting the emergence of local, private sector seed enterprises* through an integrated approach involving producer organizations, linkages to markets and value addition.
- *Coordinating linkages with other essential components of SCPI*, such as appropriate agronomic practices, soil and water management, integrated pest management, credit and marketing.

Many of those actions are already being taken in various countries and by various institutions. The challenge is to share experiences, build on the best practices that have been identified and tested, and focus on ways to adapt them to meet the specific objectives and practices of SCPI. That will ensure that the diversity required for sustainable intensification, and already available in genebanks and farmers' fields, is mobilized efficiently, effectively and in a timely manner.

Chapter 5

Water management

Sustainable intensification requires smarter, precision technologies for irrigation, and farming practices that use ecosystem approaches to conserve water

Crops are grown under a range of water management regimes, from simple soil tillage aimed at increasing the infiltration of rainfall, to sophisticated irrigation technologies and management. Of the estimated 1.4 billion ha of crop land worldwide, around 80 percent is rainfed and accounts for about 60 percent of global agricultural output[1]. Under rainfed conditions, water management attempts to control the amount of water available to a crop through the opportunistic deviation of the rainwater pathway towards enhanced moisture storage in the root zone. However, the timing of the water application is still dictated by rainfall patterns, not by the farmer.

Some 20 percent of the world's cropped area is irrigated, and produces around 40 percent of total agricultural output[1]. Higher cropping intensities and higher average yields account for this level of productivity. By controlling both the amount and timing of water applied to crops, irrigation facilitates the concentration of inputs to boost land productivity. Farmers apply water to crops to stabilize and raise yields and to increase the number of crops grown per year. Globally, irrigated yields are two to three times greater than rainfed yields. Thus, a reliable and flexible supply of water is vital for high value, high-input cropping systems. However, the economic risk is also much greater than under lower input rainfed cropping. Irrigation can also produce negative consequences for the environment, including soil salinization and nitrate contamination of aquifers.

Growing pressure from competing demands for water, along with environmental imperatives, mean that agriculture must obtain "more crops from fewer drops" and with less environmental impact. That is a significant challenge, and implies that water management for sustainable crop production intensification will need to anticipate smarter, precision agriculture. It will also require water management in agriculture to become much more adept at accounting for its water use in economic, social and environmental terms.

Prospects for sustainable intensification vary considerably across different production systems, with different external drivers of demand. In general, however, the sustainability of intensified crop production, whether rainfed or irrigated, will depend on the adoption of ecosystem approaches such as conservation agriculture, along with other key practices, including use of high-yielding varieties and good quality seeds, and integrated pest management.

Rainfed cropping systems

Many crop varieties grown in rainfed systems are adapted to exploit moisture stored in the root zone. Rainfed systems can be further improved by, for example, using deep-rooting crops in rotation, adapting crops to develop a deeper rooting habit, increasing soil water storage capacity, improving water infiltration and minimizing evaporation through organic mulching. Capture of runoff from adjacent lands can also lengthen the duration of soil moisture availability. Improving the productivity of rainfed agriculture depends largely on improving husbandry across all aspects of crop management. Factors such as pests and limited availability of soil nutrients can limit yield more than water availability *per se*[2, 3]. The principles of reduced tillage, organic mulching and use of natural and managed biodiversity (described in Chapter 2, *Farming systems*) are fundamental to improved husbandry.

The scope for implementing SCPI under rainfed conditions will depend, therefore, on the use of ecosystem-based approaches that maximize moisture storage in the root zone. While these approaches can facilitate intensification, the system is still subject to the vagaries of rainfall. Climate change will increase the risks to crop production. Nowhere is the challenge of developing effective strategies for climate change adaptation more pressing than in rainfed agriculture[4].

Other measures are needed, therefore, to allay farmers' risk aversion. They include better seasonal and annual forecasting of rainfall and water availability and flood management, both to mitigate climate change and to improve the resilience of production systems. More elaborate water management interventions are possible to reduce the production risk, but not necessarily to further intensify rainfed production. For instance, there is scope to transition some rainfed cropping systems to low-input supplementary irrigation systems, in order to bridge short dry spells during critical growth stages[5], but these are still reliant upon the timing and intensity of rainfall.

On-farm runoff management, including the use of water retaining bunds in cultivated areas, has been applied successfully in transitional climates, including the Mediterranean and parts of the Sahel, to extend soil moisture availability after each rain event. Off-farm runoff management, including the concentration of overland flow into shallow groundwater or farmer-managed storage, can allow for limited supplementary irrigation. However, when expanded over large areas, these interventions impact downstream users and overall river basin water budgets.

Extending the positive environmental and soil moisture conservation benefits of ecosystem approaches will often depend upon the level of farm mechanization, which is needed to take advantage of rainfall events. Simpler technologies, including opportunistic runoff farming, will remain inherently risky, particularly under more erratic rainfall regimes. They will also remain labour intensive.

Policymakers will need to assess accurately the relative contributions of rainfed and irrigated production at national level. If rainfed production can be stabilized by enhanced soil moisture storage, the physical and socio-economic circumstances under which this can occur need to be well identified and defined. The respective merits of low-intensity investments in SCPI across extensive rainfed systems and high intensity localized investments in full irrigation need careful socio-economic appraisal against development objectives.

With regard to institutions, there is a need for re-organization and reinforcement of advisory services to farmers dependent on rainfed agriculture, and renewed efforts to promote crop insurance for small-scale producers. A sharper analysis of rainfall patterns and soil moisture deficits will be needed to stabilize production from existing rainfed systems under climate change impacts.

Irrigated cropping systems

The total area equipped for irrigation worldwide is now in excess of 300 million ha[6], and the actual area harvested is estimated to be larger due to double and triple cropping. Most irrigation development has taken place in Asia, where rice production is practised on about 80 million ha, with yields averaging 5 tonnes per ha (compared to 2.3 tonnes per ha from the 54 million ha of rainfed lowland rice). In contrast, irrigated agriculture in Africa is practised on just 4 percent of cropped land, owing mainly to the lack of financial investment.

Irrigation is a commonly used platform for intensification because it offers a point at which to concentrate inputs. Making this *sustainable* intensification, however, depends on the location of water withdrawal and the adoption of ecosystem based approaches – such as soil conservation, use of improved varieties and integrated pest management – that are the basis of SCPI. The uniformity of distribution and the application efficiency of irrigation vary with the technology used to deliver water, the soil type and slope (most importantly its infiltration characteristic), and the quality of management.

Surface irrigation by border strip, basin or furrow is often less efficient and less uniform than overhead irrigation (e.g. sprinkler, drip, drip tape). *Micro irrigation* has been seen as a technological fix for the poor performance of field irrigation, and as a means of saving water. It is being adopted increasingly by commercial horticulturalists in both developed and developing countries, despite high capital costs.

Deficit irrigation and variants such as *regulated deficit irrigation* (RDI) are gaining hold in the commercial production of fruit trees and some field crops that respond positively to controlled water stress at critical growth stages. RDI is often practised in conjunction with micro-irrigation and "fertigation", in which fertilizers are applied directly to the region where most of the plant's roots develop. The practice has been adapted to simpler furrow irrigation in China. The benefits, in terms of reduced water inputs, are apparent but they will only be realized if the supply of water is highly reliable.

Knowledge-based precision irrigation that offers farmers reliable and flexible water application will be a major platform for SCPI. Automated systems have been tested using both solid set sprinklers and micro-irrigation, which involve using soil moisture sensing and crop canopy temperature to define the irrigation depths to be applied in different parts of the field. Precision irrigation and precision fertilizer application through irrigation water are both future possibilities for field crops and horticulture, but there are potential pitfalls. Recent computer simulations indicate that, in horticulture, salt management is a critical factor in sustainability.

The economics of irrigated agriculture are significant. The use of sprinkler and micro-irrigation technologies, as well as the automation of surface irrigation layouts, involve long term capital expenditure and operational budgets. Rain guns provide one of the cheapest capital options for large area overhead irrigation coverage, but tend to incur high operating costs. Other overhead irrigation systems have high capital costs and, without the support of production subsidies, are unsuited to smallholder cropping systems.

The service delivery of many public irrigation systems is less than optimal, owing to deficiencies in design, maintenance and management. There is considerable scope for modernizing systems and their management, through both institutional reform and the separation of irrigation service provision from broader oversight and the regulation of water resources.

Drainage is an essential, but often overlooked, complement to irrigation, especially where water tables are high and soil salinity is a constraint. Investment will be required in drainage to enhance the productivity and sustainability of irrigation systems and to ensure good management of farm inputs. However, enhanced drainage increases the risks of pollutants being exported, causing degradation in waterways and connected aquatic ecosystems.

Protected cropping, mostly in shade houses, is enjoying increasing popularity in many countries, including China and India, mainly for fruit, vegetable and flower production. In the long term, highly intensive closed cycle production systems, using conventional irrigation or hydroponic and aeroponic cultures, will become progressively more common, especially in peri-urban areas with strong markets and increasing water scarcity.

Using water for irrigation reduces instream flows, alters their timing, and creates conditions for shocks, such as toxic algal blooms. Secondary impacts include salinization and nutrient and pesticide pollution of water courses and water bodies. There are other environmental trade-offs from irrigated systems; rice paddies sequester higher levels of organic matter than dry land soils, and contribute less nitrate runoff and generate lower emissions of nitrous oxide (N_2O). Offset against this are relatively large emissions of methane (from 3 to 10 percent of global emissions) and ammonia.

Crops normally use less than 50 percent of the irrigation water they receive, and irrigation systems that lie within a fully or over-allocated river basin have low efficiency. In accounting terms, it is necessary to distinguish how much water is depleted, both beneficially and unproductively. Beneficial depletion by crops – evapotranspiration – is the intent of irrigation: ideally, transpiration would account for all depletion, with zero evaporation from soil and water surfaces. There is some potential to improve water productivity by reducing non-productive evaporative losses.

Basin level improvements in water productivity focus on minimizing non-beneficial depletion[7]. However, the downstream impacts of increased water depletion for agriculture are not neutral: there is evidence of big reductions in annual runoff from "improved" upper catchments that have adopted extensive water harvesting in parts of peninsular India[8].

Water management is a key factor in minimizing nitrogen losses and export from farms. In freely drained soils, nitrification is partially interrupted, resulting in the emission of N_2O, whereas in saturated (anoxic) conditions, ammonium compounds and urea are partially converted to ammonia, typically in rice cultivation. Atmospheric losses from urea can occur, therefore, as both ammonia and N_2O are released during wetting and drying cycles in irrigation. N is required in nitrate form for uptake at the root, but can easily move elsewhere in solution. A number of protected and slow release fertilizer compounds are under development for different situations (see Chapter 3, *Soil health*).

The dynamics of phosphate mobilization and movement in drains and waterways are complex. Phosphate export from agriculture can occur in irrigated systems if erosive flow rates are used in furrow irrigation, or if sodic soils disperse. Phosphate, and to a lesser extent nitrate, can be trapped by buffer strips located at the ends of fields and along rivers, which prevents them from reaching waterways. Hence, a combination of good irrigation management, recycling of tailwater and the incorporation of phosphate in the soil can reduce phosphate export from irrigated lands to close to zero.

The sustainability of intensified irrigated agriculture depends on minimizing off-farm externalities, such as salinization and export of pollutants, and the maintenance of soil health and growing conditions. That should be the primary focus of farm level practice, technology and decision-making, and reinforces the need for depletion water accounting and wiser water allocation at basin and catchment scales, and a better understanding of the hydrological interactions between different production systems.

Technologies that save and grow

Rainwater harvesting in Africa's Sahel[9]

A wide variety of traditional and innovative rainwater harvesting systems is found in Africa's Sahel zone. In semi-arid areas of Niger, small-scale farmers use planting pits to harvest rainwater and rehabilitate degraded land for cultivation of millet and sorghum. The technology improves infiltration and increases nutrient availability on sandy and loamy soils, leading to significant increases in yields, improved soil cover and reduced downstream flooding. Planting pits are hand-dug holes 20-30 cm in diameter and 20-25 cm deep, spaced about 1 m apart. Excavated soil is shaped into a small ridge to maximize capture of rainfall and run-off. When available, manure is added to each pit every second year. Seeds are sown directly into the pits at the start of the rainy season, and silt and sand are removed annually. Normally, the highest crop production is during the second year after manure application.

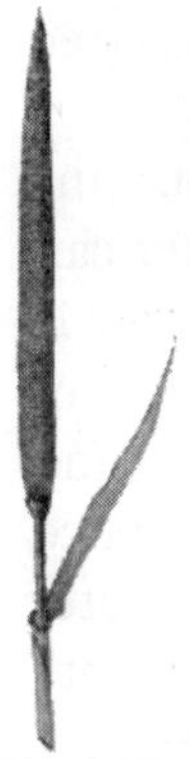

pearl millet

In eastern Ethiopia, farmers capture floodwater and runoff from ephemeral rivers, roads and hillsides using temporary stone and earth embankments. Captured water is distributed through a system of hand-dug canals up to 2 000 m long to fields of high value vegetables and fruit crops. Benefits include a 400 percent increase in gross production value from the fourth year of operation, improved soil moisture and fertility, and reduced downstream flooding.

Deficit irrigation for high yield and maximum net profits[10]

The highest crop productivity is achieved using high-yielding varieties with optimal water supply, soil fertility and crop protection. However, crops can also produce well with limited water supply. In deficit irrigation, water supply is less than the crop's full requirements, and mild stress is allowed during growth stages that are less sensitive to moisture deficiency. The expectation is that any yield reduction will be limited, and additional benefits are gained by diverting the saved water to irrigate other crops. However, use of deficit irrigation requires a clear understanding of soil-water and salt budgeting, as well as an intimate knowledge of crop behaviour, since crop response to water stress varies considerably.

A six-year study of winter wheat production on the North China Plain showed water savings of 25 percent or more through application of deficit irrigation at various growth stages. In normal years, two irrigations (instead of the usual four) of 60 mm were enough to achieve acceptably high yields and maximize net profits. In Punjab, Pakistan, a study of the long-term impacts of

cotton

deficit irrigation on wheat and cotton reported yield reductions of up to 15 percent when irrigation was applied to satisfy only 60 percent of total crop evapotranspiration. The study highlighted the importance of maintaining leaching practices in order to avoid the long-term risk of soil salinization. In studies carried out in India on irrigated groundnuts, production and water productivity were increased by imposing transient soil moisture-deficit stress during the vegetative phase, 20 to 45 days after sowing. Water stress applied during the vegetative growth phase may have had a favourable effect on root growth, contributing to more effective water use from deeper soil horizons. Higher water savings are possible in fruit trees, compared to herbaceous crops. In Australia, regulated deficit irrigation of fruit trees increased water productivity by approximately 60 percent, with a gain in fruit quality and no loss in yield.

Supplemental irrigation on rainfed dryland[11, 12]

In dry areas, farmers dependent on rainfall for cereal production can increase yields using supplemental irrigation (SI), which entails harvesting rainwater run-off, storing it in ponds, tanks or small dams, and applying it during critical crop growth stages. One of the main benefits of SI is that it permits earlier planting – while the planting date in rainfed agriculture is determined by the onset of rains, supplemental irrigation allows the date to be chosen precisely, which can improve productivity significantly. For example, in Mediterranean countries, a wheat crop sown in November has consistently higher yield and shows better response to water and nitrogen fertilizer than a crop sown in January.

The average water productivity of rain in dry areas of North Africa and West Asia ranges from about 0.35 to 1 kg of wheat grain for every cubic metre of water. ICARDA has found that, applied as supplemental irrigation and along with good management practices, the same amount of water can produce 2.5 kg of grain. The improvement is mainly attributed to the effectiveness of a small amount of water in alleviating severe moisture stress.

In the Syrian Arab Republic, SI helped boost the average grain yield from 1.2 tonnes to 3 tonnes per hectare. In Morocco, applying 50 mm of supplemental irrigation increased average yields of early planted wheat

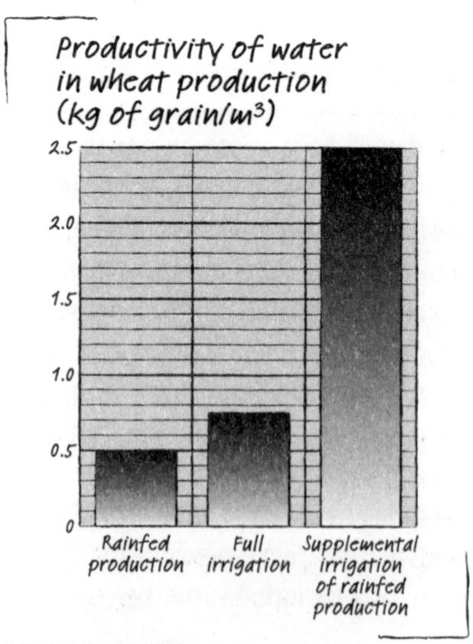

ICARDA. 2006. AARINENA water use efficiency network - Proceedings of the expert consultation meeting, 26-27 November 2006. *Aleppo, Syria.*

from 4.6 tonnes to 5.8 tonnes, with a 50 percent increase in water productivity. In Iran, a single SI application increased barley yields from 2.2 to 3.4 t/ha.

When integrated with improved varieties and good soil and nutrition management, supplemental irrigation can be optimized by deliberately allowing crops to sustain a degree of water deficit. In northern Syria, farmers applied half the amount of full SI water requirements to their wheat fields, which allowed them to double the cropped area, maximize productivity per unit of water and increase total production by one third.

Multiple uses of water systems[13]

In addition to water for crop production, irrigation systems and infrastructure can provide multiple services, including supplying water for domestic use, animal production and electricity generation, and channels for transport. Analysis by FAO of 20 irrigation schemes revealed that non-crop water uses and multiple functions of irrigation schemes are more the norm than the exception.

For example, in the Fenhe irrigation district of Shaanxi Province, China, values derived from conventional irrigation were found to be lower than those from related services, such as aquaculture, timber plantations and flood protection. The district's infrastructure, which consists of two reservoirs, three diversion dams and five main canals, was built in 1950. In recent years, Shanxi province has suffered increasing drought, flooding and water pollution, and competition for water from industrial and domestic users is growing. Owing to water shortages,

surface irrigation is now limited essentially to winter wheat and maize crops. As a result, many farmers have diversified production away from staple crops toward intensive cash crop production using mainly groundwater, and the original command area of 86 000 ha has been reduced by about 50 percent.

Within this smaller area, many more functions are serviced by the district's water allocations from the Yellow River: productive services, such as crop irrigation, aquaculture, hydropower generation, timber plantations and industrial water supply, and amenities, including flood protection, groundwater recharge and forest parkland. In this way, intensification of water use has been accompanied by conservation of environmental services.

Use of irrigation water, Fenhe district, China (percent)

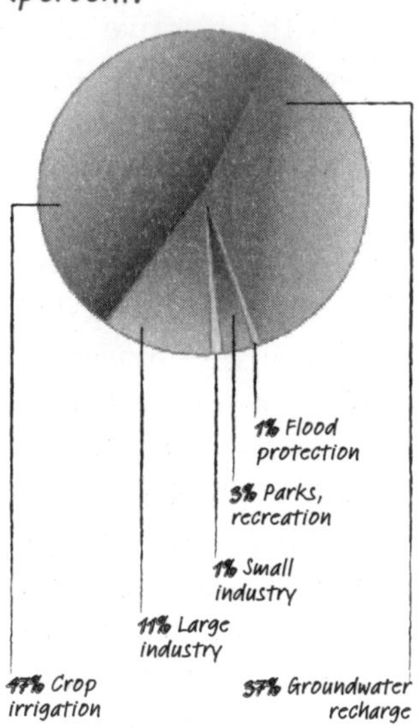

FAO. 2010. Mapping systems and service for multiple uses in Fenhe irrigation district, Shanxi Province, China. *Rome.*

The way forward

Sustainable agriculture on irrigated land – and also across the range of rainfed and improved rainfed production systems – involves trade-offs in land use, water sharing in the broadest sense, and the maintenance of supporting ecosystem services. These trade-offs are becoming more complex and have significant social, economic and political importance.

The overall governance of land and water allocations will strongly influence the scale of longer term investment in irrigated SCPI, particularly given the higher capital and input costs associated with irrigated production. Competing demands for water from other economic sectors and from environmental services and amenities will continue to grow. Water management in agriculture will need to cope with less water per hectare of land and will also have to internalize the cost of pollution from agricultural land.

With regard to policy, the nature of agriculture is changing in many countries, as the pace of rural outmigration and urbanization accelerates. Policy incentives that focus on the most pressing environmental externalities, while leveraging individual farmer's profit motives, have a greater chance of success.

For example, where agrochemical pollution of rivers and aquatic ecosystems has reached crisis point, a ban on dangerous chemicals could be accompanied by measures to raise fertilizer prices, provide farmers with objective advice on dosage rates, and remove perverse incentives to apply fertilizer excessively. Follow-up measures might promote management at "required or recommended" levels, and seek alternative approaches to higher productivity with more modest use of external inputs. In that case, more public investment would be needed to improve the monitoring of ecosystem conditions.

In the future, fertigation technology (including use of liquid fertilizers), deficit irrigation and wastewater-reuse will be better integrated within irrigation systems. While the introduction of a new technology into irrigated cropping systems has high entry costs and requires institutional arrangements for operation and maintenance, the use of precision irrigation is now global. Farmers in developing countries are already adopting low-head drip kits for niche markets, such as horticulture. In addition, the availability of cheap, plastic moulded products and plastic sheeting for plasticulture is likely to expand. However, the broad-scale adoption of alternatives, such as solar technologies, or the avoidance of polluting technologies, will need the support of regulatory measures and effective policing of compliance.

Shortcomings in governance of some irrigation investments have led to financial irregularities in capital funding, rent-seeking in management and operation, and poor co-ordination among agencies responsible for providing irrigation services to the farmer. Innovative approaches are required to create institutional frameworks that promote agricultural and water development, and at the same time safeguard the environment. There remains considerable potential to harness and learn from local initiatives in institutional development, to manage the externalities of intensification, and to reduce or avoid transaction costs. Solutions are more likely to be knowledge-rich than technology-intensive.

Chapter 6

Plant protection

Pesticides kill pests, but also pests' natural enemies, and their overuse can harm farmers, consumers and the environment. The first line of defence is a healthy agro-ecosystem

Plant pests are often regarded as an external, introduced factor in crop production. That is a misperception, as in most cases pest species occur naturally within the agro-ecosystem. Pests and accompanying species – such as predators, parasites, pollinators, competitors and decomposers – are components of crop-associated agro-biodiversity that perform a wide range of ecosystem functions. Pest upsurges or outbreaks usually occur following the breakdown of natural processes of pest regulation.

Because intensification of agricultural production will lead to an increase in the supply of food available to crop pests, pest management strategies must be an integral part of SCPI. However, they will also need to respond to concerns about the risks posed by pesticides to health and the environment. It is important, therefore, that potential pest problems associated with the implementation of SCPI are addressed through an ecosystem approach.

Although populations of potential pests are present in every crop field, every day, regular practices, such as crop monitoring and spot control measures, usually keep them in check. In fact, the total eradication of an insect pest would reduce the food supply of the pest's natural enemies, undermining a key element in system resilience. The aim, therefore, should be to manage insect pest populations to the point where natural predation operates in a balanced way and crop losses to pests are kept to an acceptable minimum.

When that approach does not seem sufficient, farmers often respond by seeking additional protection for their crops against perceived threats. The pest management decisions taken by each farmer are based on his or her individual objectives and experiences. While some may apply labour-intensive control measures, the majority turn to pesticides. In 2010, worldwide sales of pesticides were expected to exceed US$40 billion. Herbicides represent the largest market segment, while the share of insecticides has shrunk and that of fungicides has grown over the past ten years[1].

As a control tactic, over-reliance on pesticides impairs the natural crop ecosystem balance. It disrupts parasitoid and predator populations, thereby causing outbreaks of secondary pests. It also contributes to a vicious cycle of resistance in pests, which leads to further investment in pesticide development but little change in crop losses to pests, which are estimated today at 30 to 40 percent, similar to those of 50 years ago[2]. As a result, induced pest outbreaks, caused by inappropriate pesticide use, have increased[3].

Excessive use of pesticide also exposes farmers to serious health risks and has negative consequences for the environment, and sometimes for crop yields. Often less than one percent of pesticides applied actually reaches a target pest organism; the rest contaminates the air, soil and water[4].

Consumers have grown increasingly concerned about pesticide residues in food. Rapid urbanization has resulted in the expansion of urban and peri-urban horticulture, where pesticide use is more evident and its overuse even less acceptable to the public. The serious consequences of pesticide-related occupational exposure have been amply documented among farming communities, heightening social sensitivity towards agricultural workers' rights and welfare.

Public concerns are being translated into more rigorous standards both domestically and in international trade. Major retailers and supermarket chains have endorsed stricter worker welfare, food safety, traceability and environmental requirements. However, weak regulation and management of pesticides continue to undermine efforts to broaden and sustain ecologically-based pest management strategies. That is because pesticides are aggressively marketed and, therefore, often seen as the cheapest and quickest option for pest control.

Farmers would benefit from a better understanding of the functioning and dynamics of ecosystems, and the role of pests as an integral part of agro-biodiversity. Policymakers, who are often targets of complex information regarding crop pests, would also benefit from a better understanding of the real impact of pests and diseases in cropping ecosystems.

Integrated pest management

Over the past 50 years, integrated pest management (IPM) has become and remains the world's leading holistic strategy for plant protection. From its first appearance in the 1960s, IPM has been based on ecology, the concept of ecosystems and the goal of sustaining ecosystem functions[5-7].

IPM is founded on the idea that the first and most fundamental line of defence against pests and diseases in agriculture is a healthy agro-ecosystem, in which the biological processes that underpin production are protected, encouraged and enhanced. Enhancing those processes can increase yields and sustainability, while reducing input costs. In intensified systems, environmental factors of production affect the prospects for the effective management of pests:

- *Soil management* that applies an ecosystem approach, such as mulching, can provide refuges for natural enemies of pests. Building soil organic matter provides alternate food sources for generalist natural enemies and antagonists of plant disease and increases pest-regulating populations early in the cropping cycle. Addressing particular soil problems, such as salt water incursion, can render crops less susceptible to pests such as the rice stem borer.
- *Water stress* can increase the susceptibility of crops to disease. Some pests, notably weeds in rice, can be controlled by better management of water in the production system.
- *Crop varietal resistance* is essential for managing plant diseases and many insect pests. Vulnerability can arise if the genetic base of host plant resistance is too narrow.
- *Timing and spatial arrangement of crops* influence the dynamics of pest and natural enemy populations, as well as levels of pollination services for pollinator-dependent horticultural crops. As with other beneficial insects, reducing pesticide applications and increasing diversity within farms can increase the level of pollination service.

As an ecosystem-based strategy, IPM has achieved some notable successes in world agriculture. Today, large-scale government IPM programmes are operational in more than 60 countries, including Brazil, China, India and most developed countries. There is general scientific consensus – underscored by the recent International Assessment of Agricultural Science and Technology for Development[8] – that IPM works and provides the basis for protecting SCPI. The following are general principles for using integrated pest management in the design of programmes for sustainable intensification.

- *Use an ecosystem approach* to anticipate potential pest problems associated with intensified crop production. The production system should use, for example, a diverse range of pest-resistant crop varieties, crop rotations, intercropping, optimized planting time and weed management. To reduce losses, control strategies should take advantage of beneficial species of pest predators, parasites and competitors, along with biopesticides and selective, low risk synthetic pesticides. Investment will be needed in strengthening farmers' knowledge and skills.

- *Undertake contingency planning* for when credible evidence of a significant pest threat emerges. That will require investment in seed systems to support deployment of resistant varieties, and crop-free periods to prevent the carryover of pest populations to the following season. Selective pesticides with adequate regulatory supervision will need to be identified, and specific communication campaigns prepared.
- *Analyse the nature of the cause of pest outbreaks* when problems occur, and develop strategies accordingly. Problems may be caused by a combination of factors. Where the origin lies in intensification practices – for example, inappropriate plant density or ploughing that disperses weed seeds – the practices will need to be modified. In the case of invasions by pests such as locusts, methods of biological control or disease suppression used in the place of origin can be useful.
- *Determine how much production is at risk*, in order to establish the appropriate scale of pest control campaigns or activities. Infestation (not loss) of more than 10 percent of a crop area is an outbreak that demands a rapid policy response. However, risks from pests are often over-estimated, and crops can to some extent compensate physiologically for pest damage. The response should not be disproportionate.
- *Undertake surveillance to track pest patterns* in real time, and adjust response. Georeferenced systems for plant pest surveillance use data from fixed plots, along with roving survey data and mapping and analysis tools.

Approaches that save and grow

Ecosystem approaches have contributed to the success of many large-scale pest management strategies in a variety of cropping systems. For example:

Reduced insecticide use in rice

Most tropical rice crops require no insecticide use under intensification[9]. Yields have increased from 3 tonnes per ha to 6 tonnes through the use of improved varieties, fertilizer and irrigation. Indonesia drastically reduced spending on pesticide in rice production between 1988 and 2005[10]. However, in the past five years, the availability of low-cost pesticides, and shrinking support for farmers' education and field-based ecological research, have led to renewed high levels of use of pesticides and large-scale pest outbreaks, particularly in Southeast Asia[11].

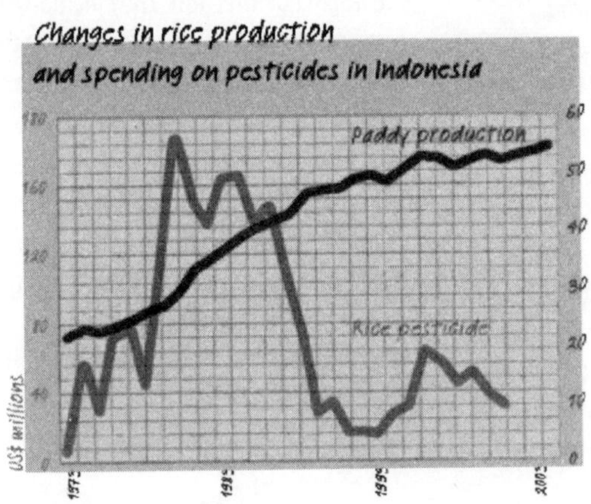

Gallagher, K.D., Kenmore, P.E. & Sogawa, K. 1994. Judicial use of insecticides deter planthopper outbreaks and extend the life of resistant varieties in Southeast Asian rice. In R.F. Denno & T.J. Perfect, eds. Planthoppers: Their ecology and management, *pp. 599-614.*

Oudejans, J.H.M. 1999. Studies on IPM policy in SE Asia: Two centuries of plant protection in Indonesia, Malaysia, and Thailand. *Wageningen Agricultural University Papers 99.1. Wageningen, the Netherlands.*

Watkins, S. 2003. The world market for crop protection products in rice. *Agrow Report. London, PJB Publications.*

Biocontrol of cassava pests

In Latin America, the centre of origin of the cassava, pest insects are normally kept under good natural population regulation. However, pests cause heavy damage when inappropriately treated with insecticides or when the crop and its pests are moved to another region, such as Africa or Asia, where effective natural enemies are absent. A biocontrol initiative led by IITA successfully brought under control the cassava green mite and the cassava mealybug throughout most of sub-Saharan Africa. This control was provided by natural enemies from Latin America, which were widely established in Africa in the 1980s and are now being introduced to Asia[12, 13].

cassava

Impact of IPM and improved agronomic practices on seed cotton production, in four districts of eastern Uganda (percent)

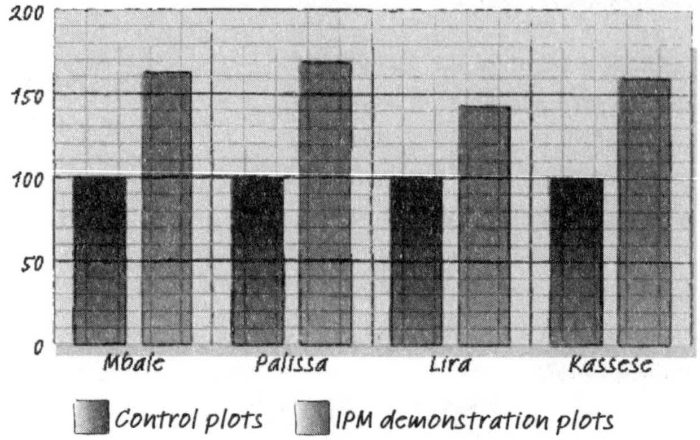

Hillocks, R., Orr, A., Riches, C. & Russell, D. 2006. Promotion of IPM for smallholder cotton in Uganda. *DFID Crop Protection Programme, Final Technical Report, Project R8403. Kent, UK, Natural Resources Institute, University of Greenwich.*

Natural enemies of cotton pests

Cotton systems have a diverse natural enemy fauna, consisting of general predators that keep sucking pests, such as white flies and leaf hoppers, under adequate natural control. Cotton's tolerance for these pests changes during the crop cycle and treatment thresholds vary according to crop stage and the extent of natural enemy presence. The mosaic of crops near cotton plays an important role in IPM systems, because neighbouring crops – such as melons, and tomatoes – can serve as sources of pests or, as in the case of fodder crops such as alfalfa, of natural enemies. In addition, effective host plant resistance conferred by transgenic Bt cotton has reduced insecticide use significantly[14].

Ecosystem approach to citrus diseases

Traditionally, growers in China and Viet Nam relied on manipulating ants to defend citrus trees from a wide range of insect pests. Recent pest outbreaks on citrus in Australia, Eritrea, Israel and the United States of America have followed excessive insecticide spraying, which disrupted naturally occurring biocontrol. While Huanglongbing disease (HLB) has not been resolved, several ecosystem approaches have slowed the impact of infection. They include certification programmes for mother trees and geographical isolation of nursery production, which is conducted in secure insect proof screen houses. In commercial plantations, insect vectors are controlled using chemical insecticides and, where applicable, biocontrol or intercropping with repellent plants such as guava. Infected trees are removed to reduce HLB inoculum sources[15, 16].

oranges

Control of viral diseases in tomatoes

tomatoes

Over the past 10 to 15 years, epidemics of viral diseases associated with high populations of whiteflies have plagued tomato production in West Africa, severely reducing yields. In some cases, tomato growing is no longer economically viable. A multipartner international public-private research collaboration helped establish in Mali an IPM programme which included an area-wide campaign to eliminate infected host plants, followed by planting of high-yielding early maturing varieties and extensive sanitation efforts that removed and destroyed tomato and pepper plants after harvest. The programme screened and evaluated new, early maturing disease-tolerant varieties, and used monthly monitoring of whitefly populations and virus incidence to assess the impact of control practices. As a result, recent tomato production was the highest in 15 years[17].

The examples above suggest various tactics that can be employed to counter or avoid plant pests in intensified production systems:

- ***Insect pests.*** It is important to conserve predators, parasitoids and beneficial pathogens to avoid secondary pest release, manage crop nutrient levels to reduce insect reproduction, deploy resistant varieties and make selective use of insecticides.
- ***Plant diseases.*** Organize seed systems that can deliver clean planting material, and deploy varieties with durable pest resistance. Use of clean irrigation water will help ensure that pathogens are not spread, while crop rotations will help suppress pathogens and support soil and root health. Farmers need to manage antagonists of plant pests to enhance biological control.
- ***Weeds.*** Management of weeds requires selective and timely manual weed control, crop rotation, cover crops, minimum tillage, intercropping and fertility management, including organic amendments. Herbicides should be used for targeted, selective control and managed so as to avoid the evolution of herbicide resistance.

The way forward

The "business as usual" approach to pest management, still followed in many countries and by many farmers, limits their potential for implementing sustainable crop production intensification. Improvements in agro-ecosystem management can help avoid indigenous pest outbreaks, respond better to pest invasions and reduce risks from pesticides to both human health and the environment. Entry points for improved ecosystem-based pest control include:

- a major pest or disease outbreak that threatens food security;
- food safety concerns arising from high levels of pesticide residues in farm produce;
- incidences of environmental pollution or human poisoning;
- striking losses of beneficial species, such as pollinators or birds;
- pesticide mismanagement, such as the proliferation of obsolete pesticide stockpiles.

In each of these cases, there is need for a pest control strategy that can be sustained and does not produce adverse side effects. After a nationally or regionally recognized pest problem has been brought under control with IPM, policymakers and technical staff are usually much more receptive to the approach, and also more willing to make the necessary policy and institutional changes to support it in the long term. The changes may include removal of pesticide subsidies, tighter enforcement of pesticide regulations, and incentives for local production of IPM inputs, such as insectaries for natural predators.

Countries should give preference to less hazardous pesticides in registration processes. They should also ensure that they apply ecologically informed decision-making to determine which pesticides may be sold and used, by whom and in what situations. Eventually, pesticide-use fees or pesticide taxes, which were pioneered in India in 1994, may be used to finance the development of alternative pest management practices and subsidize their adoption.

Policymakers can support SCPI through IPM programmes at a local, regional or national scale. They should be aware, however, that the success of effective pest management using IPM techniques depends ultimately on farmers. It is they who make key management decisions on the control of pests and diseases. Policy instruments include:

Changing perceptions of emergencies that involve pest or disease outbreaks

Perceptions	"Business as usual"	Ecosystems approach
Emergency	▶Sudden and severe pest outbreaks	▶Loss of agro-ecosystem functions resulting in severe pest outbreaks
Indicators	▶High presence of pests ▶Visual crop damage ▶Yield losses and reduced farmer incomes	▶Changes in pest population age structure ▶Emergence of pesticide resistance and abnormal outbreaks of secondary pests ▶Upward spiralling of pesticide use ▶Yield losses and diminished farmer incomes
Causes	▶Pesticide resistance ▶Appearance of new pests ▶Insufficient availability of pesticides ▶Weather conditions	▶Pesticide overuse ▶Poor crop management ▶Weather conditions ▶Emergence of new pests
Response	▶Supply more or different pesticides	▶Analysis of causes of pest problem and development of strategy for recovery of agro-ecosystem functions and rehabilitation of institutional capacity to guide recovery ▶Avoid solutions that perpetuate the problem ▶Strengthen IPM capacity through investment in human capital

- *Technical assistance and extension support* to farmers in applying ecologically based management practices and developing and adapting technologies, taking into account their local knowledge, social learning networks and conditions.
- *Targeted research* in areas such as host plant resistance to pests and diseases, practical monitoring and surveillance methods, innovative approaches to field pest management, the use of selective pesticides (including biopesticides) and biocontrol.
- *Private sector regulation*, including effective systems of governance for the registration and distribution of pesticides (specifically cov-

ered by the International Code of Conduct on the Distribution and Use of Pesticides).

- *Removal of perverse incentives* such as pesticide price or transport subsidies, the unnecessary maintenance of pesticide stocks, which encourages their use, and preferential tariffs for pesticides.

Large-scale adoption of ecosystem approaches would provide opportunities for small local industries. The scaling up of ecological pest management practices can be expected to increase demand for commercial monitoring tools, biocontrol agents such as predators, parasitoids or sterile organisms, pollination services, micro-organisms and biopesticides. Today, private companies produce more than 1000 bio-products, worth some US$590 million in 2003, based on bacteria, viruses, fungi, protozoa and nematodes[18]. This local industry would expand significantly with a shift to a more ecosystem-centric approach.

From the perspective of the food processing industry, more stable and sustainable agro-ecosystems will result in a more consistent and reliable supply of agricultural produce free of pesticide residues. Additionally, labelling food products with an IPM or similar label can help ensure access to new markets for producers.

Sustaining IPM strategies requires effective advisory services, links to research that respond to farmers' needs, support to the provision of IPM inputs, and effective regulatory control of chemical pesticide distribution and sale. One of the most effective means of promoting IPM at local level is the farmer field school, an approach that supports local learning and encourages farmers to adapt IPM technologies by drawing upon indigenous knowledge. Farmers need ready access to information on appropriate IPM inputs. The adoption of IPM can be accelerated by using, for example, cellular phones to supplement traditional methods of outreach, such as extension, media campaigns and local inputs dealers.

Chapter 7

Policies and institutions

To encourage smallholders to adopt sustainable crop production intensification, fundamental changes are needed in agricultural development policies and institutions

Unprecedented challenges to agriculture – including population growth, climate change, energy scarcity, natural resources degradation and market globalization – underscore the need to rethink policies and institutions for crop production intensification. Models used for intensification in the past have often led to costly environmental damage, and need to be revised in order to achieve greater sustainability. While "business as usual" is clearly not an option, what alternatives are available?

The focus here is on defining the conditions, policies and institutions that will enable smallholder farmers – in low-income developing economies in particular – to adopt sustainable crop production intensification. It also considers overarching issues that affect not only SCPI, but are important for the development of an agricultural sector in which SCPI is facilitated and supported. It recognizes that programmes to promote SCPI may need to go beyond "agricultural" institutions and involve other centres of policymaking.

Past experience, future scenarios

The Green Revolution was supported largely by public sector investment, with almost all of the research and development (R&D) on modern varieties being carried out in international and national research centres. Seed and agrochemicals were disseminated through government-sponsored programmes at subsidized prices.

Since the mid-1980s, the locus of agricultural research and development has shifted dramatically from the public to the private multinational sector[1]. Greater protection of intellectual property in plant innovations, rapid progress in molecular biology and the global integration of agricultural input and output markets have generated strong incentives for the private sector to invest in agricultural research and development[2]. So far, investments have targeted agriculture mainly in developed countries. Meanwhile, overall growth in public sector investment in agricultural research and development in developing countries has declined significantly. In sub-Saharan Africa, investment actually decreased during the 1990s[3].

Throughout the 1980s and until the mid-1990s, many developing countries implemented structural adjustment programmes aimed at eliminating inefficient public sector activities and allowing a dynamic private sector to reinvigorate agriculture. The results have been mixed: in many cases a dynamic private sector failed to materialize, or developed only in high potential and commercialized production, while access to agricultural services and inputs declined in more marginal areas[4]. More recently, there has been a shift towards redefining the role of the public sector to support the development of the private sector, and to provide the public goods required for development[5].

Growth in organized and globalized food value chains is another major transformation with important implications for SCPI. These chains create new income opportunities for smallholders but also generate barriers to market access. There are concerns that the concentration of market power at specific points in the chain reduces the incomes of other actors in the chain, particularly small farmers[6,7].

Considerable potential exists for improving the economic returns to farming systems while also reducing environmental and social impacts. However, that will require alternative models of agricultural technology and marketing development. Although productivity increases may be achieved faster in high-input, large-scale, specialized farming systems, the greatest scope for improving livelihood and equity exists in small-scale, diversified production systems[8].

Given the uncertainty of future demand and supply conditions, a range of scenarios for sustainable intensification in developing countries is possible. Important factors that could constitute major deviations from the baseline growth path are:

- *Climate change.* The impact of climate change on global agriculture is potentially enormous. Assessments are complex, involving projections of potential changes in climate and their impacts on production, interacting with demographic growth and dietary patterns, and market, trade and price developments[9]. A recent IFPRI analysis[10] of climate change impacts on agriculture up to 2050 indicated dramatic negative effects on productivity, with reduced food availability and human well-being in all developing regions. Together with increased demand owing to income and population growth, this was likely to contribute to a more or less significant increase in real agricultural prices between 2010 and 2050, depending on the scenario. The report estimates that public funding of at least US$7 billion annually is needed on three categories of productivity-enhancing investments – biological research, expansion of rural roads, and irrigation expansion and efficiency improvements – to compensate for the productivity losses associated with climate change by 2050. Other studies show less dramatic outcomes, with the overall impact of climate change on global food prices ranging between 7 percent and 20 percent in 2050[11]. Since agriculture is also a major source of greenhouse gas emissions, financial support and incentives to promote the adoption of low emission agricultural growth paths will become increasingly important. Reducing emissions per unit of production will be a key aspect of SCPI[12, 13].

- *Natural resources degradation.* The quality of land and water resources available for crop intensification has major implications for the design of SCPI in many areas. In the past, favourable production areas were given priority for crop intensification[14]. Increasingly, intensification will be required in more marginal areas with more variable production conditions, including soil and water quality, access to water, topography and climate. In this context, an important issue is ecosystem degradation, which reduces the availability and productivity of natural resources for SCPI. Restoration of degraded ecosystems can involve considerable expense and time, and will need long-term financing.
- *Reduction of food losses and changes in food consumption patterns.* FAO has reported post-harvest food losses of as high as 50 percent. Because action to prevent those losses would reduce the need for productivity increases, reduce costs throughout the supply chain and improve product quality, it should be part of SCPI policies and strategies. An alternative scenario, which favours environmental sustainability as well as human health, is a slowdown in growth in demand for animal products, which would reduce demand growth for feed and forage.
- *Market integration.* To be attractive to farmers, SCPI must lead to remunerative market prices. A rising trend in agricultural prices, stimulated in part by the resource constraints that are driving the move to SCPI, will enhance the profitability of investments in intensification. On the other hand, rapid productivity growth at local levels and under conditions of closed markets could generate market surpluses, driving down local prices. Price effects will also be mediated by the state of the value chain. The development of agricultural value chains must aim at enhancing smallholders' capacity for SCPI adoption and provide incentives.

Policies that save and grow

A successful strategy for sustainable intensification of crop production requires a fundamental change in the management of traditional and modern knowledge, institutions, rural investment and capacity development. Policies in all of those domains will need to provide incentives to various stakeholders and actors, especially the rural population, to participate in SCPI development.

Input and output pricing

To be profitable, SCPI requires a dynamic and efficient market for inputs and services as well as for the final produce. The prices farmers pay for inputs and are paid for agricultural outputs are perhaps the main determinant of the level, type and sustainability of crop intensification they adopt. Input prices are of particular importance for SCPI strategies, and creative policies will be needed to promote efficiency and influence technology choices. One example is the reintroduction of "market smart" subsidies, aimed at supporting the development of demand and participation in input markets using vouchers and grants. The approach seeks to avoid past problems with subsidies, such as inefficiency, negative effects on the environment, and the waste of financial resources that are needed for investments in other key public goods, such as research and rural infrastructure[5].

In contrast, environmentally harmful (or "perverse") subsidies, which encourage the use of natural resources in ways that destroy biodiversity[15], need to be carefully evaluated and, when appropriate, reformulated or removed. Perverse subsidies worldwide have been valued at from US$500 billion to US$1.5 trillion a year, and represent a powerful force for environmental damage and economic inefficiency[16].

Of course, most incentives are not designed to be "perverse" but rather to benefit a particular social or economic sector. When planning their removal, it is important, therefore, to consider the multiple objectives of incentives and to take into account the complexity of interactions among the different sectors affected positively and negatively by them[17]. Some countries have done so successfully: New Zealand abolished agricultural subsidies, starting in the 1980s[18]; Brazil has reduced livestock farming in the Amazon basin; and the Philippines has abolished fertilizer subsidies[17, 19].

Stabilization of agricultural output prices is an increasingly important condition for sustainable intensification of crop production, given the volatility experienced in commodity markets in the past few years. For farmers dependent on agricultural income, price volatility means large income fluctuations and greater risk. It reduces their capacity to invest in sustainable systems and increases the incentives to liquidate natural capital as a source of insurance.

Short-term, micro-level policies to address price volatility have frequently failed. Greater coherence at the macro policy level – for example, transparency over export availabilities and import demands – is likely to provide much more effective solutions. Reform of existing instruments, such as the Compensatory Financing Facility and the Exogenous Shock Facility of the International Monetary Fund is also needed. Through the provision of import financing or guarantees with limited conditionality, they could serve as global safety nets[18].

Seed sector regulation

Achievement of SCPI will also depend on the effective regulation of the seed sector in order to ensure farmers' access to quality seeds of varieties that meet their production, consumption and marketing conditions. Access implies affordability, availability of a range of appropriate varietal material, and having information about the adaptation of the variety[21].

Most small farmers in developing countries obtain seed from the informal seed sector, which provides traditional farmer-bred varieties and saved seeds of improved varieties. One of the main reasons farmers rely on the informal seed sector is the availability of germplasm adapted to their production conditions. Some local varieties may outperform improved varieties in marginal agricultural environments[22]. Supporting the informal sector is, therefore, one way of improving farmer access to planting material suitable for SCPI.

However, the informal seed sector lacks a viable means of informing farmers about the adaptation and production characteristics of the variety embodied in seeds, as well as their genetic purity and physical quality[23]. In some cases, the necessary information is supplied simply by observing the performance of crops in a neighbour's field. But that is not a viable option in exchanges involving strangers and non-local seed sources. Seed in formal systems is genetically uniform, is produced using scientific plant-breeding techniques, and must meet certification standards. Seed from this sector tends to be sold through specialized agro-dealers, agri-businesses or government outlets, which are subject to regulation. Any comprehensive strategy for improving farmers' access to new varieties and quality seed needs to support and expand the formal seed sector, and improve its links with the informal sector.

Payments for environmental services

The lack of market prices for ecosystem services and biodiversity means that the benefits derived from those goods are neglected or undervalued in decision-making[24]. In the agriculture sector, food prices do not incorporate all the associated costs to the environment of food production. No agencies exist to collect charges for reduced water quality or soil erosion. If farmgate prices reflected the full cost of production – with farmers effectively paying for any environmental damage they caused – food prices would probably rise. In addition to charging for agricultural disservices, policies could reward those farmers who farm sustainably through, for example, payments for environmental services (PES) schemes.

Support is growing for the use of payments for environmental services as part of the enabling policy environment for sustainable agricultural and rural development. The World Bank recommends that PES programmes be pursued by local and national governments as well as the international community[5]. PES are being integrated increasingly as a source of sustainable financing in wider rural development and conservation projects in Global Environment Facility and World Bank portfolios[25]. FAO says that demand for environmental services from agricultural landscapes will increase and PES could be an important means of stimulating their supply. However, effective deployment will depend on enabling policies and institutions at local and international levels which, in most cases, are not in place[26].

Currently, the role of PES programmes in support of sustainable agriculture is rather limited. PES initiatives have focused mainly on land diversion programmes, and there is relatively little experience with their application to agricultural production systems. To realize their benefits, PES programmes will need to cover large numbers of producers and areas, which would achieve economies of scale in transaction costs and risk management. Better integration of PES with agricultural development programmes is an important way of reducing transaction costs.

Given the limits on public finance, creative forms of alternative or additional funding from private sources will need to be developed, especially where private beneficiaries of PES can be identified. For example, a recent FAO feasibility assessment of PES in Bhutan found that the government's support for forest protection and reforestation amounted to about a third of the Ministry of Agriculture's budget[27]. Half of the funding for watershed management was assigned to plantations[28]. Were more of this investment responsibility shifted to the companies that benefit from forest protection, additional public funding could be released for under-funded activities – such as crop diversification, livestock improvement and sustainable land management – which would improve farm productivity and increase resilience to climate change[29, 30].

Agricultural investment

To engage in SCPI, the private sector – including farmers, processors and retailers – needs adequate public infrastructure and services. These are essential not only to ensure that local farming and marketing can compete with imports, but also to ensure that consumers have access to affordable, locally produced food. It is particularly important that governments ensure low transaction costs for input acquisition, produce marketing, and access to natural resources, information, training, education and social services. That will require adequate funding for both maintenance and net investment.

The agricultural sector in developing countries will need substantial and sustained investment in human, natural, financial and social capital in order to achieve SCPI. According to FAO estimates, total average annual gross investment of US$209 billion, at constant 2009 prices, is needed in primary agriculture (such as soil fertility, farm machinery and livestock) and in downstream sectors (storage, marketing and processing) in order to achieve the production increases needed by 2050. Public investment would also be needed in agricultural research and development, rural infrastructure and social safety nets[21].

Current investment in the agriculture of developing countries is clearly insufficient. Inadequate levels of domestic funding have been exacerbated by the reduction in Official Development Assistance to agriculture since the late 1980s. Together, these shortfalls have led over the last two decades to a drastic decline in capital for agricultural development. If SCPI is to succeed, agricultural investment must be significantly increased.

Funding for climate change adaptation and mitigation is highly relevant to SCPI. For example, one key means of adapting to climate change – increasing resilience in agricultural production systems through the use of new varieties generated by expanded plant breeding and seed systems – is an essential component of sustainable intensification. SCPI could thus benefit from funding allocated to climate change adaptation. Sustainable intensification could also play an important role in climate change mitigation, through increased carbon sequestration in sustainably managed soils and reduction of emissions owing to more efficient use of fertilizer and irrigation.

At present, there is no international agreement or framework for channelling mitigation funding on a significant scale to agriculture in developing countries. However, it is one area of discussion in the UNFCCC negotiations within the context of developing countries' Nationally Appropriate Mitigation Actions[12, 21].

Enabling institutions

A lack of institutional capacity and functioning is a common constraint on agriculture in developing countries, and limits the effectiveness of policies at local level. Institutions for SCPI will have two basic functions: to ensure the necessary quantity and quality of key resources – natural resources, inputs, knowledge and finance – and to ensure that small farmers have access to those resources. In the following, institutions are divided into two main categories: those related to key resources for SCPI, and those that influence the functioning of agricultural product markets, including value chains.

Access to key resources

Land. The shift to SCPI requires improvements in soil fertility, erosion control and water management. Farmers will undertake them only if they are entitled to benefit, for a sufficiently long period, from the increase in the value of natural capital. Often, however, their rights are poorly defined, overlapping or not formalized. Improving the land and water rights of farmers – especially those of women, who are increasingly the ones making production decisions – is a key incentive to adoption of sustainable intensification.

Land tenure programmes in many developing countries have focused on formalizing and privatizing rights to land, with little regard for customary and collective systems of tenure. Governments should give greater recognition to such systems, as growing evidence indicates that, where they provide a degree of security, they can also provide effective incentives for investments[31]. However, customary systems that are built on traditional social hierarchies may be inequitable and fail to provide the access needed for sustainable intensification. While there is no single "best practice" model for recognizing customary land tenure, recent research has outlined a typology for selecting alternative policy responses based on the capacity of the customary tenure system[32].

Plant genetic resources. Crop improvement is fundamental to SCPI. During the Green Revolution, the international system that generated new crop varieties was based on open access to plant genetic resources. Today, national and international policies increasingly support the privatization of PGR and plant breeding through the use of intellectual property rights (IPRs). The number of countries that provide legal protection to plant varieties has grown rapidly in response to the WTO Agreement on Trade Related Aspects of Intellectual Property Rights, which stipulates that members must offer protection through "patents or an effective *sui generis* system"[33].

Plant variety protection systems typically grant a temporary exclusive right to the breeders of a new variety to prevent others from reproducing and selling seed of that variety. They range from patent systems with rather restrictive rules to the more open system under the International Union for the Protection of New Varieties of Plants, which contains the so-called "breeders' exemption", whereby "acts done for the purpose of breeding other varieties are not subject to any restriction".

IPRs have stimulated rapid growth in private sector funding of agricultural research and development. Only 20 years ago, most R&D was carried out by universities and public laboratories in industrialized countries and generally available in the public domain. Investment is now concentrated in six major companies[34]. There is evidence of a growing divide between a small group of countries with high levels of R&D investments and a large number with very low levels[3, 35]. More importantly, technology spillovers from industrialized to developing countries are driven by research agendas that are oriented towards commercial prospects rather than maximum public good.

Increasing concentration in the private plant breeding and seed industry, and the high costs associated with developing and patenting biotechnology innovations, raise further concerns that the introduction of inappropriate IPRs will restrict access to the plant genetic resources needed for new plant breeding initiatives in the public sector[34, 36]. It has been argued that decentralized ownership of IPRs and high transactions costs can lead to an "anti-commons" phenomenon in which innovations with fragmented IPRs are underused, thus impeding the development of new varieties[37].

Mechanisms are needed, therefore, to safeguard access to plant genetic resources for SCPI, at both global and national levels. The emerging global system for the conservation and use of plant genetic resources will provide the necessary international framework (see Chapter 4, *Crops and varieties*). There are several kinds of national IPR regime, with varying degrees of obligations and access[38]. Countries should adopt IPR systems that ensure access of their national breeding programmes to the plant genetic resources needed for SCPI.

Research. Applied agricultural research must become much more effective in facilitating major transformations in land use and cropping systems for SCPI. Many agricultural research systems are not sufficiently development-oriented, and have often failed to integrate the needs and priorities of the poor in their work. Research systems are often under-resourced, and even some that are well-funded are not sufficiently connected with the broader processes of development[39]. The following are the most important steps needed for strengthening research for SCPI:

- *Increase funding.* The decline of public investment in agricultural R&D needs to be reversed. Funding for the CGIAR Centers and national research systems must be substantially enhanced, and linkages between public and private sector research strengthened.
- *Strengthen research systems, starting at local levels.* To generate solutions that are relevant, acceptable and attractive to local populations, research on SCPI practices must start at the local and national levels, with support from the global level. While important, the research efforts of the CGIAR "can neither substitute, nor replace the complex and routine strategizing, planning, implementing, problem-solving and learning needed on multiple fronts, which only national institutions and actors can and must do"[39]. There is a huge, underutilized potential to link farmers' traditional knowledge with science-based innovations, through favourable institutional arrangements. The same holds for the design, implementation and

monitoring of improved natural resource management that links community initiatives to external expertise.

- *Focus research on SCPI in both high and low potential areas.* High-potential areas will continue to be major providers of food in many countries. However, the productive capacity of land and water resources is reaching its limits in some areas, and will not be sufficient to guarantee food security. Therefore, much of future growth in food production will need to take place in so-called low potential or marginal areas, which are home to hundreds of millions of the poorest and most food insecure people. SCPI and related rural employment offer the most realistic prospects for improving those people's nutrition and livelihoods.
- *Give priority to research that benefits smallholders.* In low-income, food importing countries, small-scale producers, farm workers and consumers can benefit directly from SCPI research focused on staple food crops, which have a comparative advantage. Priority should also go to agricultural productivity growth and natural resources conservation in heavily populated marginal areas, diversification to higher value products in order to increase and stabilize farmers' incomes, and improved practices that increase returns to labour of landless and near-landless rural workers[40].
- *Learn from failures and successes.* A recent IFPRI study of proven successes in agricultural development[10] highlights the breeding of rust-resistant wheat and improved maize worldwide, improved cassava varieties in Africa, farmer-led "re-greening of the Sahel" in Burkina Faso (see Chapter 3, *Soil health*), and zero-tillage on the Indo-Gangetic Plain (see Chapter 2, *Farming systems*). Those successes were the result of a combination of factors, including sustained public investment, private incentives, experimentation, local evaluation, community involvement and dedicated leadership. In all cases, science and technology were a determinant.
- *Link research with extension.* Solutions to the problems of low productivity and degradation of natural resources are needed at large scale, but replication of SCPI practices is constrained by the vast range and diversity of site-specific conditions. Linking local, national and international research and site-specific extension services is, therefore, particularly important. To be relevant for the advancement of SCPI, research and extension systems must work together with farmers in addressing multiple challenges.

Technologies and information. Successful adoption of SCPI will depend on the capacity of farmers to make wise technology choices, taking into account both short- and long-term implications. Farmers also need to have a good understanding of the role of agro-ecosystem functions. The wealth of traditional knowledge held by farmers and local communities all over the world has been widely documented, in particular by the report of the International Assessment of Agricultural Knowledge, Science and Technology for Development[8]. Institutions are needed to protect this knowledge and to facilitate its exchange and use in SCPI strategies.

Institutions must also ensure farmers' access to relevant external knowledge and help link it to traditional knowledge. Rural advisory and agricultural extension services were once the main channel for the flow of new knowledge to – and, in some cases, from – farmers. However, public extension systems in many developing countries have long been in decline, and the private sector has failed to meet the needs of low-income producers[12]. The standard, public sector and supply-driven model of agricultural extension, based on technology transfer and delivery, has all but disappeared in many countries, particularly in Latin America[41].

Extension has been privatized and decentralized, with activities now involving a wide array of actors, such as agribusiness companies, non-governmental organizations (NGOs), producer organizations and farmer-to-farmer exchanges, and new channels of communication, including mobile phones and the Internet[42]. One key lesson from this experience is that the high transactions costs of individual extension contacts are a major barrier to reaching small and low-income producers. Advisory services to support SCPI will need to build upon farmer organizations and networks, and public-private partnerships[12].

FAO promotes farmer field schools as a participatory approach to farmer education and empowerment. The aim of the FFS is to build farmers' capacity to analyse their production systems, identify problems, test possible solutions and adopt appropriate practices and technologies. Field schools have been very successful in Asia and sub-Saharan Africa, notably in Kenya and Sierra Leone, where they cover a broad range of farming activities, including marketing, and have proved to be sustainable even without donor funding.

To make wise decisions about what to plant and where and when to sell, farmers need access to reliable information about market prices, including medium-term trends. Government market information services suffer many of the same weaknesses as extension services[43]. There is now renewed donor and commercial interest in market information, taking advantage of SMS messaging and the Internet.

Financial resources for farmers. Credit will be essential for creating the technical and operational capacities needed for SCPI. In particular, longer term loans are needed for investment in natural capital, such as soil fertility, that will increase efficiency, promote good agricultural practices and boost production. Although many new types of institutions – such as credit unions, savings cooperatives and micro-finance institutions – have spread to the rural areas of developing countries in recent years, the majority of small farmers have limited or no access to them. The inability of local financial institutions to offer longer term loans, coupled with farmers' lack of collateral, hampers sustainable crop intensification.

Insurance would encourage farmers to adopt production systems that are potentially more productive and more profitable, but involve greater financial risk. In recent years, pilot crop insurance programmes have been introduced as a risk management tool in many rural communities in developing countries. Index insurance products – where indemnities are triggered by a measurable weather event, such as drought or excess rain, rather than by an assessment of losses in the field – have found enthusiastic support among donors and governments. Assessments by IFAD and the World Food Programme of 36 weather-based index insurance pilot programmes have demonstrated their potential as a risk-management tool[44].

Alternatives to insurance, especially the accumulation of savings and other saleable assets, are often overlooked. Also, preventive, on-farm measures and instruments to reduce exposure to risk should be seriously considered.

Productive social safety nets. Social safety net programmes include cash transfers and distribution of food, seeds and tools[45]. They ensure access to a minimum amount of food and other vital social services. Recent initiatives include Ethiopia's Productive Safety Net Programme and the Kenya Hunger Safety Net Programme. There is debate about whether such programmes risk creating dependency and weakening local markets. However, recent evidence indicates that trade-offs between protection and development are not pronounced[46]. Instead, safety net programmes can be a form of social investment in human capital (for example, nutrition and education) and productive capital, allowing households to adopt higher risk strategies aimed at achieving higher productivity[27].

Policymakers need to understand the determinants of vulnerability at the household level and to design productive safety nets that offset the downward spiral of external shocks and coping strategies. The latter include selling assets, reducing investments in natural resources and taking children out of school, all of which undermine sustainability. Safety nets are also increasingly being linked to rights-based approaches to food security[47].

Agricultural marketing institutions and value chains

Growth of the food marketing sector offers new opportunities for smallholder farmers by broadening their choice of input suppliers and of outlets for produce, as well as increasing their access to credit and training[48, 49]. However, access to both input and output markets has proved problematic for many smallholders, who remain at the margins of the new agricultural economy[50-53].

How smallholders fit into a specific agricultural value chain depends largely on the underlying cost structures of the chain and of their farm production processes[54]. The primary cost advantage of smallholders is their ability to supply low-cost labour for labour-intensive crops. When smallholders have no apparent comparative advantage, agribusinesses may seek alternative structures for organizing production, such as vertical integration or buying directly from large holders. In those cases, the challenge is to create comparative advantages for smallholders or to reduce the transaction costs associated with purchasing from large numbers of farmers producing small quantities. To forge links to high-value markets, small farmers need to be organized in institutions that reduce transaction costs, and given access to information on market requirements[48, 49, 54, 55].

Contract farming provides mechanisms of vertical coordination between farmers and buyers, which allows for an evident degree of assurance in some of the main negotiation parameters: price, quality, quantity and time of delivery[56]. While farmers have benefited from contractual agreements, substantial evidence suggests that the smallest farmers are often unable to enter formal arrangements[55]. Improving the legal and institutional framework of contracts would dramatically reduce transaction costs[55, 57]. However, farm consolidation, resulting from increased off-farm rural employment or migration to urban areas, appears inevitable.

Small farmer access to markets can also be improved through better organization and greater cooperation, which may involve not only farmers but also a larger number of stakeholders, including agricultural support service providers, NGOs, researchers, universities, local government and international donors. One example is the *Plataforma de concertación* in Ecuador, which has helped farmers to achieve higher yields and gross margins, while reducing the use of toxic pesticides. Nevertheless, its self-financing capability has still to be verified[54].

The way forward

From the outset, policymakers should take a long, hard look at past and current experiences in order to identify clear options and steps that need to be taken now to foster sustainable crop production intensification. There is no "one-size-fits-all" set of recommendations for choosing the most appropriate policies and institutions. However, it is possible to identify the key features of a supporting policy and institutional environment for SCPI:

- *Linking public and private sector support.* The private sector and civil society have an important role to play in increasing the availability of investment funds, promoting greater efficiency and accountability of institutions, and ensuring a participatory and transparent policy process. Resource mobilization should take into consideration the full range of services and products that SCPI can generate. Payments for environmental services generated by a sustainable production system may prove to be an important source of investment resources.
- *Incorporating the value of natural resources and ecosystem services into agricultural input and output price policies.* That can be achieved by establishing realistic environmental standards, eliminating perverse incentives, such as subsidies on fertilizer and pesticides, and by creating positive incentives, such as payments for environmental services, or environmental labelling in value chains.

- *Increasing coordination and reducing transaction costs.* Involving small farmers in SCPI development requires coordinated action to reduce the transaction costs of access to input and output markets, extension and payments for environmental services. Institutions and technologies that facilitate participation – including farmer groups, community organizations, customary forms of collective action, and modern communication technologies – are therefore a key requirement for SCPI.
- *Building regulatory, research and advisory systems for a very wide range of production and marketing conditions.* SCPI represents a shift from a highly standardized and homogeneous model of agricultural production to regulatory frameworks that allow for and encourage heterogeneity – for example, by including informal seed systems in seed regulatory policies and integrating traditional knowledge into research and extension.
- *Recognizing and incorporating customary access and management practices into SCPI initiatives.* Assessing and strengthening the current capacity of customary systems of access to the inputs needed for SCPI, and of indigenous systems of agricultural management, will both be important.

Policies and programmes for sustainable crop production intensification will cut across a number of sectors and involve a variety of stakeholders. Therefore, a strategy for achieving sustainable intensification needs to be a cross-cutting component of a national development strategy. An important step for policymakers in achieving SCPI adoption is to initiate a process of embedding or mainstreaming strategies for sustainable intensification in national development objectives. SCPI should be an integral part of country-owned development programmes, such as Poverty Reduction Strategy Processes and food security strategies and investments, including follow-ups to the commitments to support food security made at the Group of 8 summit in L'Aquila, Italy, in 2009.

The roll-out of SCPI agendas and plans in developing countries requires concerted action at international and national levels, with the participation of governments, the private sector and civil society. Multi-stakeholder processes are now considered the key to food security at all levels. At the global level, FAO and its development partners will play an important supporting role.

Sources

Chapter 1: The challenge

1. FAO. 2004. *The ethics of sustainable agricultural intensification.* FAO Ethics Series, No. 3. pp. 3-5. Rome.

2. Kassam, A. & Hodgkin, T. 2009. *Rethinking agriculture: Agrobiodiversity for sustainable production intensification.* Platform for Agrobiodiversity Research (http://agrobiodiversityplatform.org/climatechange/2009/05/14/rethinking-agriculture-agrobiodiversity-for-sustainable-production-intensification/).

3. Royal Society. 2009. *Reaping the benefits: Science and the sustainable intensification of global agriculture.* RS Policy document 11/09. London.

4. Hazell, P.B.R. 2008. *An assessment of the impact of agricultural research in South Asia since the green revolution.* Rome, Science Council Secretariat.

5. Gollin, D., Morris, M. & Byerlee, D. 2005. Technology adoption in intensive post-green revolution systems. *Amer. J. Agr. Econ.*, 87(5): 1310-1316.

6. Tilman, D. 1998. The greening of the green revolution. *Nature*, 396: 211-212. DOI: 10.1038/24254

7. World Bank. 2007. *World Development Report 2008.* Washington, DC, International Bank for Reconstruction and Development and World Bank.

8. FAO. 2011. FAOSTAT statistical database (http://faostat.fao.org/).

9. FAO. 2009. *The State of Food Insecurity in the World: Economic crises – impacts and lessons learned.* Rome.

10. Bruinsma, J. 2009. *The resource outlook to 2050: By how much do land, water and crop yields need to increase by 2050?* Paper presented at the FAO Expert Meeting on How to Feed the World in 2050, 24–26 June 2009. Rome, FAO.

11. Tilman, D., Cassman, K.G., Matson, P.A., Naylor, R. & Polasky, S. 2002. Agricultural sustainability and intensive production practices. *Nature*, 418: 671–677.

12. FAO. 2010. *The State of Food Insecurity in the World: Addressing food insecurity in protracted crises.* Rome.

13. FAO. 2009. *Food security and agricultural mitigation in developing countries: Options for capturing synergies.* Rome.

14. IFAD. 2010. *Rural Poverty Report 2011. New realities, new challenges: New opportunities for tomorrow's generation.* Rome.

15. United Nations. *World urbanization prospects, the 2009 revision population database* (http://esa.un.org/wup2009/unup/).

16. Rosegrant, M.W., Ringler, C. & Msangi, S. 2008. *International model for policy analysis of agricultural commodities and trade (IMPACT): Model description.* Washington, DC, IFPRI.

17. FAO. 2003. *World agriculture: Towards 2015/2030*, by J. Bruinsma, ed. UK, Earthscan Publications Ltd and Rome, FAO.

18. FAO. 2009. *Feeding the world, eradicating hunger.* Background document for World Summit on Food Security, Rome, November 2009. Rome.

19. Nellemann, C., MacDevette, M., Manders, T., Eickhout, B., Svihus, B., Prins, A.G. & Kaltenborn, B.P., eds. 2009. *The environmental food crisis – The environment's role in averting future food crises. A UNEP rapid response assessment.* Norway, United Nations Environment Programme and GRID-Arendal.

20. IPCC. 2001. *Climate Change 2001: Synthesis report. A contribution of working groups I, II, and III to the Third Assessment Report of the Intergovernmental Panel on Climate Change*, by R.T. Watson & the Core Writing Team, eds. UK, Cambridge and New York, NY, USA, Cambridge University Press.

21. IPCC. 2007. *Climate Change 2007: Synthesis Report. An assessment of the intergovernmental panel on climate change.* Geneva, Switzerland.

22. Rosenzweig, C. & Tubiello, F.N. 2006. Adaptation and mitigation strategies in agriculture: An analysis of potential synergies. *Mitigation and adaptation strategies for global change*, 12: 855-873.

23. Jones, P. & Thornton, P. 2008. Croppers to livestock keepers: Livelihood transitions to 2050 in Africa due to climate change. *Environmental Science & Policy*, 12(4): 427-437.

24. Burney, J.A., Davis, S.J. & Lobell, D.B. 2010. Greenhouse gas mitigation by agricultural intensification. *Proc. Natl. Acad. Sci.*, 107(26): 12052-12057.

25. FAO. 2010. *Price volatility in agricultural markets: Evidence, impact on food security and policy responses.* Economic and Social Perspectives Policy Brief No. 12. Rome.

26. Nelson, G.C., Rosegrant, M.W., Palazzo, A., Gray, I., Ingersoll, C., Robertson, R., Tokgoz, S., Zhu, T., Sulser, T.B., Ringler, C., Msangi, S. & You, L. 2010. *Food security, farming, and climate change to 2050: Scenarios, results, policy options.* Washington, DC, IFPRI.

27. FAO. 2006. *World agriculture: Towards 2030/2050. An FAO perspective.* Rome.

28. EC. 2007. *Food security thematic programme: Thematic strategy paper and multiannual indicative programme 2007-2010.* Brussels.

29. Godfray, C., Beddington, J.R., Crute, I.R., Haddad, L., Lawrence, D., Muir, J.F., Pretty, J., Robinson, S., Thomas, S.M. & Toulmin, C. 2010. Food security: The challenge of feeding 9 billion people. *Science,* 327: 812-818.

30. FAO. 2010. *Report of the twenty-second session of the Committee on Agriculture, Rome, 29 November – 3 December 2010.* Rome.

31. FAO. 2010. *Sustainable crop production intensification through an ecosystem approach and an enabling environment: Capturing efficiency through ecosystem services and management.* Rome.

32. Foresight. 2011. *The future of food and farming: Challenges and choices for global sustainability.* Final Project Report. London, the Government Office for Science.

33. IAASTD. 2009. *Agriculture at the crossroads,* by B.D. McIntyre, H.R. Herren, J. Wakhungu & R.T. Watson, eds. Washington, DC.

34. Pretty, J.N., Noble, A.D., Bossio, D., Dixon, J., Hine, R.E., de Vries, F. & Morison, J.I.L. 2006. Resource-conserving agriculture increases yields in developing countries. *Environ. Sci. Technol.,* 40: 1114–1119.

35. Badgley, C., Moghtader, J., Quintero, E., Zakem, E., Chappell, M., Aviles-Vazquez, K., Samulon, A. & Perfecto, I. 2007. Organic agriculture and the global food supply. *Renew. Agric. Food Syst.,* 22: 86–108.

36. Power, A.G. 2010. Ecosystem services and agriculture: Tradeoffs and synergies. *Phil. Trans. R. Soc. B.,* 365(1554): 2959-2971.

37. Warner, K.D. 2006. Extending agroecology: Grower participation in partnerships is key to social learning. *Renewable Food Agric. Syst.,* 21(2): 84-94.

38. Swanson, B.E. & Rajalahti, R. 2010. *Strengthening agricultural extension and advisory systems: Procedures for assessing, transforming, and evaluating extension systems.* Agriculture and Rural Development Discussion Paper 45. Washington, DC, The International Bank for Reconstruction and Development and World Bank.

39. FAO. 2011. *The State of Food and Agriculture: Women in agriculture – Closing the gender gap for development.* Rome.

Chapter 2: Farming systems

1. Doran, J.W. & Zeiss, M.R. 2000. Soil health and sustainability: Managing the biotic component of soil quality. *Applied Soil Ecology,* 15: 3–11.

2. Pretty, J. 2008. Agricultural sustainability: Concepts, principles and evidence. *Phil Trans Royal Society of London,* B 363(1491): 447-466.

3. Kassam, A.H., Friedrich, T., Shaxson, F. & Pretty, J. 2009. The spread of Conservation Agriculture: Justification, sustainability and uptake. *Int. Journal of Agric. Sust.,* 7(4): 292-320.

4. Godfray, C., Beddington, J.R., Crute, I.R., Haddad, L., Lawrence, D., Muir, J.F., Pretty, J., Robinson, S., Thomas, S.M. & Toulmin, C. 2010. Food security: The challenge of feeding 9 billion people. *Science,* 327: 812-818.

5. Pretty, J., Toulmin, C. & Williams, S. 2011. Sustainable intensification in African agriculture. *Int. Journal of Agric. Sust.,* 9.1. (in press)

6. Shaxson, F., Kassam, A., Friedrich, T., Boddey, R. & Adekunle, A. 2008. *Underpinning the benefits conservation agriculture: Sustaining the fundamental of soil health and function.* Main document for the Workshop on Investing in Sustainable Crop Intensification: The case of soil health, 24-27 July. Rome, FAO.

7. Uphoff, N., Ball, A.S., Fernandes, E., Herren, H., Husson, O., Laing, M., Palm, C., Pretty, J., Sanchez, P., Sanginga, N. & Thies, J., eds. 2006. *Biological approaches to sustainable soil systems.* Boca Raton, Florida, USA, CRC Press, Taylor & Francis Group.

8. Montgomery, D. 2007. *Dirt, the erosion of civilizations.* Berkeley and Los Angeles, USA, University California Press.

9. FAO. 2003. *World agriculture: Towards 2015/2030,* by J. Bruinsma, ed. UK, Earthscan Publications Ltd and Rome, FAO.

10. Mrema, G.C. 1996. *Agricultural development and the environment in Sub-Saharan Africa: An engineer's perspective.* Keynote paper presented at the First International Conference of SEASAE, Oct. 2-4, 1996, Arusha, Tanzania.

11. Legg, B.J., Sutton, D.H. & Field, E.M. 1993. *Feeding the world: Can engineering help?* Fourth Erasmus Darwin Memorial Lecture, 17 November 1993, Silsoe.

12. Baig, M.N. & Gamache, P.M. 2009. *The economic, agronomic and environmental impact of no-till on the Canadian prairies.* Canada, Alberta Reduced Tillage Linkages.

13. Lindwall, C.W. & Sonntag, B., eds. 2010. *Landscape transformed: The history of conservation tillage and direct seeding.* Saskatoon, Canada, Knowledge Impact in Society.

14. Friedrich, T. & Kienzle, J. 2007. *Conservation agriculture: Impact on farmers' livelihoods, labour, mechanization and equipment.* Rome, FAO.

15. Giller, K.E., Murmiwa, M.S., Dhliwayo, D.K.C., Mafongoya, P.L. & Mpepereki, S. 2011. Soyabeans and sustainable agriculture in Southern Africa. *Int. Journal of Agric. Sust.,* 9(1). (in press)

16. Knuutila, O., Hautala, M., Palojarvi, A. & Alakukku, L. 2010. Instrumentation of automatic measurement and modelling of temperature in zero tilled soil during whole year. In: *Proceedings of the International Conference on Agricultural Engineering AgEng 2010, Towards Environmental Technologies, Clermont Ferrand, France, Sept. 6-8.* France, Cemagref.

17. Owenya, M.Z., Mariki, W.L., Kienzle, J., Friedrich, T. & Kassam, A. 2011. Conservation agriculture (CA) in Tanzania: The case of Mwangaza B CA farmer field school (FFS), Rhotia Village, Karatu District, Arusha. *Int. Journal of Agric. Sust.,* 9.1. (in press)

18. Bruce, S.E., Howden, S.M., Graham, S., Seis, C., Ash, J. & Nicholls, A.O. 2005. Pasture cropping: Effect on biomass, total cover, soil water & nitrogen. *Farming Ahead.*

19. Landers, J. 2007. Tropical crop-livestock systems in Conservation Agriculture: The Brazilian experience. *Integrated Crop Management*, 5. Rome, FAO.

20. Joshi, P.K., Challa, J. & Virmani, S.M., eds. 2010. *Conservation agriculture: Innovations for improving efficiency, equity and environment.* New Delhi, New Delhi National Academy of Agricultural Sciences.

21. IFPRI. 2010. Zero tillage in the rice-wheat systems of the Indo-Gangetic Plains: A review of impacts and sustainability implications, by O. Erenstein. *In* D.J. Spielman & R. Pandya-Lorch, eds. *Proven successes in agricultural development: A technical compendium to millions fed.* Washington, DC.

22. Sims, B., Friedrich, T., Kassam, A.H. & Kienzle, J. 2009. *Agroforestry and conservation agriculture: Complementary practices for sustainable agriculture.* Paper presented at the 2nd World Congress on Agroforestry, Nairobi, August 2009. Rome.

23. Kassam, A., Stoop, W. & Uphoff, N. 2011. Review of SRI modifications in rice crop and water management and research issues for making further improvements in agricultural and water productivity. *Paddy and water environment*, 9.

Chapter 3: Soil health

1. Hettelingh, J.P., Slootweg, J. & Posch, M., eds. 2008. *Critical load, dynamic modeling and impact assessment in Europe: CCE Status Report 2008.* The Netherlands, Netherlands Environmental Assessment Agency.

2. Cassman, K.G., Olk, D.C. & Dobermann, A., eds. 1997. Scientific evidence of yield and productivity declines in irrigated rice systems of tropical Asia. *International Rice Commission Newsletter*, 46. Rome, FAO.

3. de Ridder, N., Breman, H., van Keulen, H. & Stomph, T.J. 2004. Revisiting a "cure against land hunger": Soil fertility management and farming systems dynamics in the West Africa Sahel. *Agric. Syst.*, 80(2): 109–131.

4. Fermont, A.M., van Asten, P.J.A., Tittonell, P., van Wijk, M.T. & Giller, K.E. 2009. Closing the cassava yield gap: An analysis from smallholder farms in East Africa. *Field Crops Research*, 112: 24-36.

5. Howeler, R.H. 2002. Cassava mineral nutrition and fertilization. *In* R.J. Hillocks, M.J. Thresh & A.C. Bellotti, eds. *Cassava: Biology, production and utilization*, pp. 115-147. Wallingford, UK, CABI Publishing.

6. Allen, R.C. 2008. The nitrogen hypothesis and the English agricultural revolution: A biological analysis. *The Journal of Economic History*, 68: 182-210.

7. FAO. 2011. FAOSTAT statistical database (http://faostat.fao.org/).

8. Jenkinson, D.S. Department of Soil Science, Rothamsted Research. Interview with BBC World. 6 November 2010.

9. Miao, Y., Stewart, B.A. & Zhang, F.S. 2011. Long-term experiments for sustainable nutrient management in China. A review. *Agron. Sustain. Dev.* (in press)

10. Bot, A. & Benites, J. 2005. *The importance of soil organic matter: Key to drought-resistant soil and sustained food and production.* FAO Soil Bulletin No. 80. Rome.

11. Dudal, R. & Roy, R.N. 1995. *Integrated plant nutrition systems.* FAO Fertilizer and Plant Nutrition Bulletin No. 12. Rome.

12. Roy, R.N., Finck, A., Blair, G.J. & Tandon, H.L.S. 2006. *Plant nutrition for food security. A guide for integrated nutrient management.* FAO Fertilizer and Plant Nutrition Bulletin 16. Rome.

13. Karlen, D.L., Mausbach, M.J., Doran, J.W., Cline, R.G., Harris, R.F. & Schuman, G.E. 1997. Soil quality: A concept, definition and framework for evaluation. *Soil Sci. Soc. Am. J.*, 61: 4-10.

14. USDA-NRCS. 2010. *Soil quality - Improving how your soil works* (http://soils.usda.gov/sqi/).

15. EU-JRC. 2006. *Bio-Bio project: Biodiversity-Bioindication to evaluate soil health*, by R.M. Cenci & F. Sena, eds. Institute for Environment and Sustainability. EUR, 22245.

16. Kinyangi, J. 2007. *Soil health and soil quality: A review.* Ithaca, USA, Cornell University. (mimeo)

17. Vanlauwe, B., Bationo, A., Chianu, J., Giller, K.E., Merckx, R., Mokwunye, U., Ohiokpehai, O., Pypers, P., Tabo, R., Shepherd, K.D., Smaling, E.M.A., Woomer, P.L. & Sanginga, N. 2010. Integrated soil fertility management - Operational definition and consequences for implementation and dissemination. *Outlook on Agriculture*, 39:17-24.

18. Bationo, A. 2009. Soil fertility – Paradigm shift through collective action. *Knowledge for development – Observatory on science and technology* (http://knowledge.cta.int/en/Dossiers/Demanding-Innovation/Soil-health/Articles/Soil-Fertility-Paradigm-shift-through-collective-action).

19. IFDC. 2011. *Integrated soil fertility management* (www.ifdc.org/getdoc/1644daf2-5b36-4191-9a88-ca8a4aab93cb/ISFM).

20. Rodale Institute. *Soils* (http://rodaleinstitute.org/course/M2/1).

21. FAO. 2008. An international technical workshop Investing in sustainable crop intensification: The case for improving soil health, FAO, Rome: 22-24 July 2008. *Integrated Crop Management*, 6(2008). Rome.

22. Weber, G. 1996. Legume-based technologies for African savannas: Challenges for research and development. *Biological Agriculture and Horticulture*, 13: 309-333.

23. Chabi-Olaye, A., Nolte, C., Schulthess, F. & Borgemeister, C. 2006. Relationships of soil fertility and stem borers damage to yield in maize-based cropping system in Cameroon. *Ann. Soc. Entomol. (N.S.)*, 42 (3-4): 471-479.

24. Giller, K.E., Beare, M.H., Lavelle, P., Izac, A. & Swift, M.J. 1997. Agricultural intensification, soil biodiversity and agroecosystem function. *Applied Soil Ecology*, 6: 3-16.

25. Sanchez, P.A., Shepherd, K.D., Soule, M.J., Place, F.M., Buresh, R.J., Izac, A.-M.N., Mokwunye, A.U., Kwesiga, F.R., Ndiritu, C.G. & Woomer, P.L. 1997. Soil fertility replenishment in Africa: An investment. *In* R.J. Buresh, P.A. Sanchez & F. Calhoun, eds. *Replenishing soil fertility in Africa: Proceedings of an international symposium, 6 November 1996*, pp. 1-46. Madison and Indianapolis, USA, Soil Science Society of America Inc.

26. Sanginga, N. & Woomer, P.L. 2009. *Integrated soil fertility management in Africa: Principles, practices, and developmental processes.* Nairobi, TSBF-CIAT.

27. Sanginga, N., Dashiell, K.E., Diels, J., Vanlauwe, B., Lyasse, O., Carsky, R.J., Tarawali, S., Asafo-Adjei, B., Menkir, A., Schulz, S., Singh, B.B., Chikoye, D., Keatinge, D. & Ortiz, R. 2003. Sustainable resource management coupled to resilient germplasm to provide new intensive cereal–grain–legume–livestock systems in the dry savanna. *Agriculture, Ecosystems and Environment*, 100: 305-314.

28. Sanchez, P.A. 2000. Linking climate change research with food security and poverty reduction in the topics. *Agriculture, Ecosystems and Environment*, 82: 371-383.

29. Garrity, D.P., Akinnifesi, F.K., Ajayi, O.C., Weldesemayat, S.G., Mowo, J.G., Kalinganire, A., Larwanou, M. & Bayala, J. 2010. Evergreen agriculture: A robust approach to sustainable food security in Africa. *Food Security*, 2: 197-214.

30. Dobermann, A. 2000. Future intensification of irrigated rice systems. *In* J.E. Sheehy, P.L. Mitchel, & B. Hardy, eds. *Re-designing rice photosynthesis to increase yield*, pp. 229-247. Makati City, Philippines and Amsterdam, IRRI / Elsevier.

31. Byrnes, B.H., Vlek, P.L.C. & Craswell, E.T. 1979. The promise and problems of super granules for rice fertilization. *In* S. Ahmed, H.P.M. Gunasena & Y.H. Yang, eds. *Proceedings: Final inputs review meeting, Honolulu, Hawaii, 20-24 August 1979*. Hawaii, East-West Center.

32. Craswell, E.T., De Datta, S.K., Obcemea, W.N. & Hartantyo, M. 1981. Time and mode of nitrogen fertilizer application. *Fertilizer Research*, 2: 247-259.

33. Rong-Ye, C. & Zhu Zhao Liang. 1982. Characteristics of the fate and efficiency of nitrogen in supergranules of urea. *Fertilizer Research*, 3: 63-71.

34. Roy, R.N. & Misra, R.V. 2003. Economic and environmental impact of improved nitrogen management in Asian rice. *In* FAO. *Sustainable rice production for food security. Proceedings of the 20th Session of the International Rice Commission. Bangkok, 23-26 July 2002*. Rome.

35. Thomas, J. & Prasad, R. 1982. On the nature of mechanism responsible for the higher efficiency for urea super granules for rice. *Plant and Soil*, 69: 127-130.

36. Visocky, M. 2010. Fertilizer system revolutionizes rice farming in Bangladesh. *Frontlines*, 12(2010).

37. Peng, S., Buresh, R.J., Huang, J., Zhong, X., Zou, Y., Yang, J., Wang, G., Liu, Y., Hu, R., Tang, Q., Cui, K., Zhang, F.S. & Dobermann, A. 2010. Improving nitrogen fertilization in rice by site-specific N management. A review. *Agron. Sustain. Dev.*, 30(2010): 649–656.

38. Sachs, J., Remans, R., Smukler, S., Winowiecki, L., Sandy, J., Andelman, S.J., Cassman, K.G., Castle, L.D., DeFries, R., Denning, G., Fanzo, J., Jackson, L.E., Leemans, R., Lehmann, J., Milder, J.C., Naeem, S., Nziguheba, G., Palm, C.A., Pingali, P.L., Reganold, J.P., Richter, D.D., Scherr, S.J., Sircely, J., Sullivan, C., Tomich, T.P. & Sanchez, P.A. 2010. Monitoring the world's agriculture. *Nature*, 466: 558-560.

39. Steiner, K., Herweg, K. & Dumanski, J. 2000. Practical and cost-effective indicators and procedures for monitoring the impacts of rural development projects on land quality and sustainable land management. *Agriculture, Ecosystems and Environment*, 81: 147-154.

40. FAO. 2010. *Climate-smart agriculture: Policies, practices and financing for food security, adaptation and mitigation.* Rome.

41. Dumanski, J. & Pieri, C. 2000. Land quality indicators: Research plan. *Agriculture, Ecosystems & Environment*, 81: 93-102.

42. Mutsaers, H.J.W. 2007. *Peasants, farmers and scientists.* New York, USA, Springer Verlag.

Chapter 4: Crops and varieties

1. Fowler, C. & Hodgkin, T. 2004. Plant genetic resources for food and agriculture: Assessing global availability. *Annu. Rev. Envirn. Resour.*, 29: 143-79.

2. FAO. 2010. *The Second Report on the State of the World's Plant Genetic Resources for Food and Agriculture.* Rome.

3. Alexandrova, N. & Atanassov, A. 2010. *Agricultural biotechnologies in developing countries: Options and opportunities in crops, forestry, livestock, fisheries and agro-industry to face the challenges of food insecurity and climate change (ABDC-10).* Issue paper for the Regional session for Europe and Central Asia – Agricultural biotechnologies in Europe and Central Asia: New challenges and opportunities in a view of recent crises and climate change, Guadalajara, Mexico, 1-4 March 2010.

4. FAO. 2009. *Declaration of the World Summit on Food Security,16-18 November 2009.* Rome.

5. FAO. 2009. *International Treaty on Plant Genetic Resources for Food and Agriculture: A global treaty for food security and sustainable agriculture.* Rome.

6. CBD. 2006. *Global Biodiversity Outlook* 2. Montreal, Canada.

7. Moore, G. & Tymowski, W. 2005. *Explanatory guide to the International Treaty for Plant Genetic Resources for Food and Agriculture.* Gland, Switzerland, Cambridge, UK and Bonn, Germany, IUCN.

8. Jarvis, D., Hodgkin, T., Bhuwon, S., Fadda, C. & Lopez Noriega, I. 2011. *A heuristic framework for identifying multiple ways of supporting the conservation and use of traditional crop varieties within the agricultural production systems. Critical reviews in plant sciences.* (in press)

9. Hunter, D. & Heywood, V., eds. 2011. *Crop wild relatives. A manual of in situ conservation.* London, Bioversity International, Earthscan.

10. Street, K., Mackay, M., Zeuv, E., Kaul, N., El Bouhssine, M., Konopka, J. & Mitrofanova, O. 2008. *Swimming in the gene pool – A rational approach to exploiting large genetic resource collections. Proceedings 11th International Wheat Genetics Symposium, Brisbane.* Sydney, Sydney University Press.

11. Ceccarelli, S., Grando, S., Shevstov, V., Vivar, H., Yayaoui, A., El-Bhoussini, M. & Baum, M. 2001. *The ICARDA strategy for global barley improvement.* Aleppo, Syria, ICARDA.

12. Lipper, L., Anderson, C.L. & Dalton, T.J., eds. 2010. *Seed trade in rural markets: Implications for crop diversity and agricultural development.* Rome, FAO and London, Earthscan.

Chapter 5: Water management

1. IIASA/FAO. 2010. *Global agro-ecological zones (GAEZ v3.0).* Laxenburg, Austria, IIASA and Rome, FAO.

2. French, R.J. & Schultz, J.E. 1984. Water use efficiency of wheat in a Mediterranean type environment. I: The relation between yield, water use and climate. *Australian Journal of Agricultural Research,* 35(6): 743–764.

3. Sadras, V.O. & Angus, J.F. 2006. Benchmarking water use efficiency of rainfed wheat in dry environments. *Australian Journal of Agricultural Research,* 57: 847–856.

4. UNDP. 2006. *Human Development Report 2006.* New York, USA.

5. Wani, S.P., Rockstrom, J. & Oweis, T., eds. 2009. Rainfed agriculture: Unlocking the potential. *Comprehensive Assessment of Water Management in Agriculture* 7. Wallingford, UK, CABI Publishing.

6. FAO. 2011. AQUASTAT statistical database (www.fao.org/nr/water/aquastat/main/index.stm).

7. Perry, C., Steduto, P., Allen, R. & Burt, C. 2009. Increasing productivity in irrigated agriculture: Agronomic constraints and hydrological realities. *Agricultural Water Management,* 96(2009): 1517–1524.

8. Batchelor, C., Singh, A., Rama Rao, M.S. & Butterworth, J. 2005. *Mitigating the potential unintended impacts of water harvesting.* UK, Department for International Development.

9. Liniger, H.P., Mekdaschi Studer, R., Hauert, C. & Gurtner, M. 2011. *Sustainable land management in practice – Guidelines and best practices for Sub-Saharan Africa.* Rome, TerrAfrica, WOCAT and FAO.

10. FAO. 2002. *Deficit irrigation practices.* Water reports No. 32, 51: 87-92.

11. Oweis, T., Hachum, A. & Kijne, J. 1999. *Water harvesting and supplemental irrigation for improved water use efficiency in dry areas.* SWIM Paper 7. Colombo, Sri Lanka, ICARDA/IMWI.

12. ICARDA. 2010. *ICARDA Annual Report 2009.* Aleppo, Syria.

13. FAO. 2010. *Mapping systems and service for multiple uses in Fenhe irrigation district, Shanxi Province, China.* Rome.

Chapter 6: Plant protection

1. Rana, S. 2010. *Global agrochemical market back in growth mode in 2010.* Agrow (www.agrow.com).

2. Lewis, W.J., van Lenteren, J.C., Phatak, S.C. & Tumlinson, III, J.H. 1997. A total system approach to sustainable pest management. *Proc. Natl. Acad. Sci.,* 94(1997): 12243–12248.

3. Wood, B.J. 2002. Pest control in Malaysia's perennial crops: A half century perspective tracking the pathway to integrated pest management. *Integrated Pest Management Reviews,* 7: 173-190.

4. Pimentel, D. & Levitan, L. 1986. Pesticides: Amounts applied and amounts reaching pests. *BioScience,* 36(2): 86-91.

5. Stern, V.M., Smith, R.F., van den Bosch, R. & Hagen, K.S. 1959. The integrated control concept. *Hilgardia,* 29: 81-101.

6. FAO. 1966. *Proceedings of the FAO Symposium on Integrated Pest Control, Rome, 1965.* Rome, FAO.

7. Smith, R.F. & Doutt, R.L. 1971. The pesticide syndrome–diagnosis and suggested prophylaxis. *In* C.B. Huffaker, ed. *Biological Control. AAAS Symposium Proceedings on Biological Control, Boston, December 1969,* pp. 331-345. New York, Plenum Press.

8. IAASTD. 2009. *Agriculture at the crossroads,* by B.D. McIntyre, H.R. Herren, J. Wakhungu & R.T. Watson, eds. Washington, DC.

9. Way, M.J. & Heong, K.L. 1994. The role of biodiversity in the dynamics and management of insect pests of tropical irrigated rice: A review. *Bulletin of Entomological Research,* 84: 567-587.

10. Gallagher, K., Ooi, P., Mew T., Borromeo, E., Kenmore, P.E. & Ketelaar, J. 2005. Ecological basis for low-toxicity: Integrated pest management (IPM) in rice and vegetables. *In* J. Pretty, ed. *The Pesticide Detox,* pp. 116-134. London, Earthscan.

11. Catindig, J.L.A., Arida, G.S., Baehaki, S.E., Bentur, J.S., Cuong, L.Q., Norowi, M., Rattanakarn, W., Sriratanasak, W., Xia, J. & Lu, Z. 2009. *In* K.L. Heong & B. Hardy, eds. *Planthoppers: New threats to the sustainability of intensive rice production systems in Asia,* pp.191- 220, 221-231. Los Baños, Philippines, IRRI.

12. Neuenschwander, P. 2001. Biological control of the cassava mealybug in Africa: A review. *Biological Control,* 21(3): 214-229.

13. Bellotti, A.C., Braun, A.R., Arias, B., Castillo, J.A. & Guerrero, J.M. 1994. Origin and management of neotropical cassava arthropod pests. *African Crop Science Journal,* 2(4): 407-417.

14. Luttrell, R.G., Fitt, G.P., Ramalho, F.S. & Sugonyaev, E.S. 1994. Cotton pest management: Part 1. A worldwide perspective. *Annual Review of Entomology*, 39: 517-526.

15. Bove, J.M. 2006. Huanglongbing: A destructive, newly-emerging, century-old disease of citrus. *Journal of Plant Pathology*, 88(1): 7-37.

16. Gottwald, T.R. 2010. Current epidemiological understanding of Citrus Huanglongbing. *Annual Review of Phytopathology*, 48: 119-139.

17. Gilbertson, R.L. 2006. *Integrated pest management of tomato virus diseases in West Africa* (www.intpdn.org/files/IPM Tomato Bob Gilbertson UC Davis.pdf).

18. Guillon, M. 2004. *Current world situation on acceptance and marketing of biological control agents (BCAS).* Pau, France, International Biocontrol Manufacturer's Association.

Chapter 7: Policies and institutions

1. Pingali, P. & Raney, T. 2005. *From the green revolution to the gene revolution: How will the poor fare?* ESA Working Paper No. 05-09. Rome, FAO.

2. Pingali, P. & Traxler, G. 2002. *Changing locus of agricultural research: Will the poor benefit from biotechnology and privatization trends.* Food Policy, 27: 223-238.

3. Beintema, N.M. & Stads, G.J. 2010. *Public agricultural R&D investments and capacities in developing countries: Recent evidence for 2000 and beyond.* Note prepared for GCARD 2010.

4. Crawford, E., Kelley, V., Jayne, T. & Howard, J. 2003. *Input use and market development in Sub-Saharan Africa: An overview.* Food Policy, 28(4): 277-292.

5. World Bank. 2007. *World Development Report 2008.* Washington, DC, International Bank for Reconstruction and Development and World Bank.

6. De Schutter, O. 2010. *Addressing concentration in food supply chains: The role of competition law in tackling the abuse of buyer power.* UN Special Rapporteur on the right to food, Briefing note 03. New York, USA.

7. Humphrey, J. & Memedovic, O. 2006. *Global value chains in the agrifood sector.* Vienna, UNIDO.

8. IAASTD. 2009. *Agriculture at the crossroads,* by B.D. McIntyre, H.R. Herren, J. Wakhungu & R.T. Watson, eds. Washington, DC.

9. Alexandratos, N. 2010. *Expert meeting on "Feeding the World in 2050". Critical evaluation of selected projections.* Rome, FAO. (mimeo)

10. IFPRI. 2010. *Proven successes in agricultural development: A technical compendium to Millions Fed,* by D.J. Spielman & R. Pandya-Lorch, eds. Washington, DC.

11. Fischer, R.A., Byerlee, D. & Edmeades, G.O. 2009. *Can technology deliver on the yield challenge to 2050?* Paper presented at the FAO Expert Meeting: How to Feed the World in 2050, 24-26 June 2009. Rome, FAO.

12. FAO. 2010. *Climate smart agriculture: Policies, practices and financing for food security, adaptation and mitigation.* Rome.

13. FAO. 2009. *Food security and agricultural mitigation in developing countries: Options for capturing synergies.* Rome.

14. Hazell, P. & Fan, S. 2003. *Agricultural growth, poverty reduction and agro-ecological zones in India: An ecological fallacy?* Food Policy, 28(5-6): 433-436.

15. CBD. 2010. *Perverse incentives and their removal or mitigation* (www.cbd.int/incentives/perverse.shtml).

16. UNEP/IISD. 2000. *Environment and trade: A handbook.* Canada, IISD.

17. OECD. 2003. *Perverse incentives in biodiversity loss.* Paper prepared for the Ninth Meeting of the Subsidiary Body on Scientific, Technical and Technological Advice (SBSTTA 9). Paris.

18. Rhodes, D. & Novis, J. 2002. *The impact of incentives on the development of plantation forest resources in New Zealand.* Information Paper No. 45. New Zealand Ministry of Agriculture and Forestry.

19. DNR. 2008. *Environmental harmful subsidies - A threat to biodiversity.* Munich, Germany.

20. FAO. 2010. *Price volatility in agricultural markets: Evidence, impact on food security and policy responses.* Economic and Social Perspectives Policy Brief No. 12. Rome.

21. FAO. 2009. *Feeding the world, eradicating hunger.* Background document for World Summit on Food Security, Rome, November 2009. Rome.

22. Ceccarelli, S. 1989. Wide adaptation. How wide? *Euphytica,* 40: 197-205.

23. Lipper, L., Anderson, C.L. & Dalton, T.J. 2009. *Seed trade in rural markets: Implications for crop diversity and agricultural development.* Rome, FAO and London, Earthscan.

24. TEEB. 2010. *The economics of ecosystems and biodiversity: Mainstreaming the economics of nature: A synthesis of the approach, conclusions and recommendations of TEEB.* Malta, Progress Press.

25. Wunder, S., Engel, S.Y. & Pagiola, S. 2008. Payments for environmental services in developing and developed countries. *Ecological economics,* 65(4): 663-852.

26. FAO. 2007. *The State of Food and Agriculture 2007: Paying farmers for environmental services.* Rome.

27. FAO. 2010. *The State of Food Insecurity in the World: Addressing food insecurity in protracted crises.* Rome.

28. GNHC. 2009. *10th five year plan 2008-2013.* Main document, vol. I. Royal Government of Bhutan.

29. Wilkes, A., Tan, J. & Mandula. 2010. The myth of community and sustainable grassland management in China. *Frontiers of Earth Science in China,* 4(1): 59–66.

30. Lipper, L. & Neves, B. 2011. Pagos por servicios ambientales: ¿qué papel ocupan en el desarrollo agrícola sostenible? *Revista Española de Estudios Agrosociales y Pesqueros,* 228(7-8): 55-86.

31. Donnelly, T. 2010. *A literature review on the relationship between property rights and investment incentives.* Rome, FAO. (mimeo)

32. Fitzpatrick, D. 2005. Best practice: Options for the legal recognition of customary tenure. *Development and Change*, 36(3): 449–475. DOI: 10.1111/j.0012-155X.2005.00419.x

33. FAO. 2010. *The Second Report on the State of the World's Plant Genetic Resources for Food and Agriculture*. Rome.

34. Piesse, J. & Thirtle, C. 2010. Agricultural R&D, technology and productivity. *Phil. Trans. R. Soc. B.*, 365(1554): 3035-3047.

35. Pardey, P.G., Beintema, N., Dehmer, S. & Wood, S. 2006. *Agricultural research: A growing global divide?* IFPRI Food Policy Report. Washington, DC, IFPRI.

36. United Nations. 2009. *Promotion and protection of human rights: Human rights questions, including alternative approaches for improving the effective enjoyment of human rights and fundamental freedoms* (UN GA Doc A/64/170). New York, USA.

37. Wright, B.D., Pardey, P.G., Nottenberg, C. & Koo, B. 2007. Agricultural innovation: Investments and incentives. *In* R.E. Evenson & P. Pingali, eds. *Handbook of agricultural economics*, vol. 3. Amsterdam, Elsevier Science.

38. Helfer, L.H. 2004. *Intellectual property rights in plant varieties*. Rome, FAO.

39. GAT. 2010. *Transforming agricultural research for development*. Paper commissioned by the Global Forum on International Agricultural Research (GFAR) as an input into the Global Conference on Agricultural Research for Development (GCARD), Montpellier, 28-31 March 2010.

40. Hazell, P., Poulton, C., Wiggins, S. & Dorward, A. 2007. *The future of small farms for poverty reduction and growth*. 2020 Discussion Paper No. 42. Washington, DC, International Food Policy Research Institute.

41. IFAD. 2010. *Rural Poverty Report 2011. New realities, new challenges: New opportunities for tomorrow's generation*. Rome.

42. Scoones, I. & Thompson, J. 2009. *Farmer first revisited: Innovation for agricultural research and development*. Oxford, ITDG Publishing.

43. Shepherd, A.W. 2000. *Understanding and using market information*. Marketing Extension Guide, No. 2. Rome, FAO.

44. IFAD/WFP. 2010. *The potential for scale and sustainability in weather index insurance for agriculture and rural livelihoods*, by P. Hazell, J. Anderson, N. Balzer, A. Hastrup Clemmensen, U. Hess & F. Rispoli. Rome.

45. Devereux, S. 2002. Can social safety nets reduce chronic poverty? *Development Policy Review*, 20(5): 657-675.

46. Ravallion, M. 2009. *Do poorer countries have less capacity for redistribution?* Policy Research Working Paper No. 5046. Washington, DC, World Bank.

47. FAO. 2006. *The right to food guidelines: Information papers and case studies*. Rome.

48. Shepherd, A.W. 2007. *Approaches to linking producers to markets*. Agricultural Management, Marketing and Finance Occasional Paper, No. 13. Rome, FAO.

49. Winters, P., Simmons, P. & Patrick, I. 2005. Evaluation of a hybrid seed contract between smallholders and a multinational company in East Java, Indonesia. *The Journal of Development Studies*, 41(1): 62–89.

50. Little, P.D. & Watts, M.J., eds. 1994. *Living under contract: Contract farming and agrarian transformation in Sub-Saharan Africa*. Madison, USA, University of Wisconsin Press.

51. Berdegué, J., Balsevich, F., Flores, L. & Reardon, T. 2003. *Supermarkets and private standards for produce quality and safety in Central America: Development implications*. Report to USAID under the RAISE/SPS project, Michigan State University and RIMISP.

52. Reardon, T., Timmer, C.P., Barrett, C.B. & Berdegué, J. 2003. The rise of supermarkets in Africa, Asia, and Latin America. *American Journal of Agricultural Economics*, 85(5): 1140-1146.

53. Johnson, N. & Berdegué, J.A. 2004. *Collective action and property rights for sustainable development: Property rights, collective action, and agribusiness*. IFPRI Policy Brief, 2004. Washington, DC.

54. Cavatassi, R., Gonzalez, M., Winters, P.C., Andrade-Piedra, J., Thiele, G. & Espinosa, P. 2010. *Linking smallholders to the new agricultural economy: The case of the Plataformas de Concertación in Ecuador*. ESA Working Paper, No. 09-06. Rome, FAO.

55. McCullogh, E.B., Pingali, P.L. & Stamoulis, K.G., eds. 2008. *The transformation of agri-food systems: Globalization, supply chains and smallholder farmers*. Rome, FAO and London, Earthscan.

56. Singh, S. 2002. Multi-national corporations and agricultural development: A study of contract farming in the Indian Punjab. *Journal of International Development*, 14: 181–194.

57. Dietrich, M. 1994. *Transaction cost economics and beyond: Towards a new economics of the firm*. London, Routledge.

Abbreviations

CA conservation agriculture
CBD Convention on Biological Diversity
CGIAR Consultative Group on International Agricultural Research
DNR Deutscher Naturschutzring
EC European Commission
EU-JRC European Commission - Joint Research Centre
FAO Food and Agriculture Organization of the United Nations
FFS farmer field school
GAT Global Authors' Team
GNHC Gross National Happiness Commission
ha hectares
HLB Huanglongbing disease
IAASTD International Assessment of Agricultural Knowledge, Science and Technology for Development
ICARDA International Centre for Agricultural Research in the Dry Areas
ICRAF World Agroforestry Centre
IFAD International Fund for Agricultural Development
IFDC International Fertilizer Development Center
IFPRI International Food Policy Research Institute
IIASA International Institute for Applied Systems Analysis
IISD International Institute for Sustainable Development
IITA International Institute of Tropical Agriculture
IPCC Intergovernmental Panel on Climate Change
IPM integrated pest management
IPR intellectual property right
IRRI International Rice Research Institute
ITPGRFA International Treaty on Plant Genetic Resources for Food and Agriculture
N nitrogen
N_2O nitrous oxide
NGOs non-governmental organizations
OECD Organisation for Economic Co-operation and Development
P phosphorus
PES payments for environmental services
PGR plant genetic resources
PGRFA plant genetic resources for food and agriculture
RDI regulated deficit irrigation
R&D research and development
SCPI sustainable crop production intensification
SI supplemental irrigation
SMS short message service
SSNM site-specific nutrient management
t tonnes
TEEB The Economics of Ecosystems and Biodiversity
UDP urea deep placement
UN United Nations
UNDP United Nations Development Programme
UNEP United Nations Environment Programme
UNFCCC United Nations Framework Convention on Climate Change
UPOV International Union for the Protection of New Varieties of Plants
USDA-NRCS United States Department of Agriculture - Natural Resources Conservation Service
USG urea super granules
WFP World Food Programme
WTO World Trade Organization